TOSEL®

HIGH JUNIOR

 International TOSEL Committee

GRAMMAR 2

CONTENTS

BROCHURES

TOSEL 소개	TOSEL Level Chart	4
	About **TOSEL** - TOSEL에 관하여	6
	Why **TOSEL** - 왜 TOSEL인가	8
	Evaluation - 평가	9
	Grade Report - 성적표 및 인증서	10
Grammar Series 소개	Grammar Series 특장점	12
	Grammar Series Level	13
	70분 학습 Guideline	14

High Junior 1권

I. 문장의 형성	Unit 1	8품사와 문장성분	21
	Unit 2	문장의 형식	31
	Unit 3	문장의 배열	41
	Unit 4	문장의 강조	51
	TOSEL	실전문제 1	61
II. 부정사와 동명사	Unit 1	원형부정사	69
	Unit 2	to부정사	79
	Unit 3	동명사	89
	Unit 4	to부정사구와 동명사구	99
	TOSEL	실전문제 2	109
III. 분사	Unit 1	현재분사	117
	Unit 2	과거분사	127
	Unit 3	분사구문	137
	Unit 4	독립분사구문	147
	TOSEL	실전문제 3	157

High Junior 2권

IV. 수동태	Unit 1	수동태의 형성	21
	Unit 2	수동태와 능동태의 전환	31
	Unit 3	수동태와 전치사의 사용	41
	Unit 4	주의해야 할 수동태 용법	51
	TOSEL	실전문제 4	61
V. 관계대명사와 관계부사	Unit 1	관계대명사의 사용	69
	Unit 2	관계대명사와 선행사	79
	Unit 3	관계대명사의 생략	89
	Unit 4	관계부사	99
	TOSEL	실전문제 5	109
VI. 가정법	Unit 1	가정법 현재와 과거	117
	Unit 2	가정법 과거완료	127
	Unit 3	혼합가정법	137
	Unit 4	특수가정법	147
	TOSEL	실전문제 6	157

TOSEL® Level Chart · TOSEL 단계표

COCOON
아이들이 접할 수 있는 공식 인증 시험의 첫 단계로써, 아이들의 부담을 줄이고 즐겁게 흥미를 유발할 수 있도록 컬러풀한 색상과 디자인으로 시험지를 구성하였습니다.

Pre-STARTER
친숙한 주제에 대한 단어, 짧은 대화, 짧은 문장을 사용한 기본적인 문장표현 능력을 측정합니다.

STARTER
흔히 접할 수 있는 주제와 상황과 관련된 주제에 대한 짧은 대화 및 짧은 문장을 이해하고 일상생활 대화에 참여하며 실질적인 영어 기초 의사소통 능력을 측정합니다.

BASIC
개인 정보와 일상 활동, 미래 계획, 과거의 경험에 대해 구어와 문어의 형태로 의사소통을 할 수 있는 능력을 측정합니다.

JUNIOR
일반적인 주제와 상황을 다루는 회화와 짧은 단락, 실용문, 짧은 연설 등을 이해하고 간단한 일상 대화에 참여하는 능력을 측정합니다.

HIGH JUNIOR
넓은 범위의 사회적, 학문적 주제에서 영어를 유창하고 정확하게, 효과적으로 사용할 수 있는 능력 및 중문과 복잡한 문장을 포함한 다양한 문장구조의 사용 능력을 측정합니다.

ADVANCED
대학 및 대학원에서 요구되는 영어능력과 취업 또는 직업근무환경에 필요한 실용영어 능력을 측정합니다.

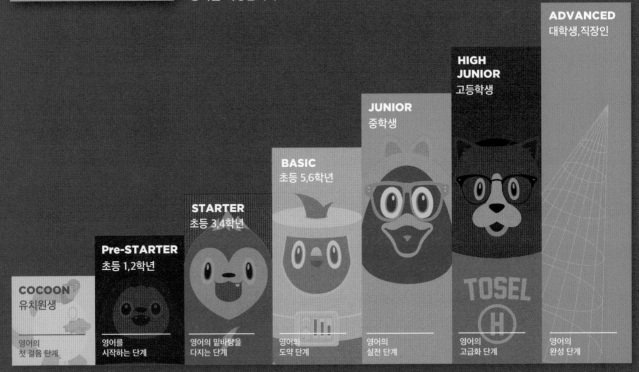

COCOON 유치원생 — 영어의 첫 걸음 단계.
Pre-STARTER 초등 1,2학년 — 영어를 시작하는 단계
STARTER 초등 3,4학년 — 영어의 밑바탕을 다지는 단계
BASIC 초등 5,6학년 — 영어의 도약 단계
JUNIOR 중학생 — 영어의 실전 단계
HIGH JUNIOR 고등학생 — 영어의 고급화 단계
ADVANCED 대학생,직장인 — 영어의 완성 단계

TOSEL
교재 Series

TOSEL LEVEL	Age	Vocabulary Frequency	Readability Score	교과 과정 연계	Grammar	VOCA	Reading	Listening
Cocoon	K5-K7	500	0-1	Who is he? (국어 1단원 1-1)	There is · There are	150	Picking Pumpkins (Phonics Story)	Phonics
Pre-Starter	P1-P2	700		How old are you? (통합교과 1-1)	be + adjective	300	Me & My Family (Reading series Ch.1)	묘사하기
Starter	P3-P4	1000-2000	1-2	Spring, Summer, Fall, Winter (통합교과 3-1)	Simple Present	800	Ask More Questions (Reading Series Ch.1)	날씨/시간 표현
Basic	P5-P6	3000-4000	3-4	Show and Tell (사회 5-1)	Superlative	1700	Culture (Reading Series Ch.3)	상대방 의견 묻고 답하기
Junior	M1-M2	5000-6000	5-6	중 1, 2 과학, 기술가정	to-infinitive	4000	Humans and Animals (Reading Series Ch.1)	정보 묻고 답하기
High Junior	H1-H3			고등학교 - 체육	2nd Conditional	7000	Health (Reading Series Ch.1)	사건 묘사하기

■ TOSEL의 세분화된 레벨은 각 연령에 맞는 어휘와 읽기 지능 및 교과 과정과의 연계가
가능하도록 설계된 교재들로 효과적인 학습 커리큘럼을 제공합니다.

■ TOSEL의 커리큘럼에 따른 학습은
정확한 레벨링 → 레벨에 적합한 학습 → 영어 능력 인증 시험 TOSEL에서의 공신력 있는 평가를 통해
진단 → 학습 → 평가의 선순환 구조를 실현합니다.

About TOSEL®

TOSEL은 각급 학교 교과과정과 연령별 인지단계를 고려하여 단계별 난이도와 문항으로
영어 숙달 정도를 측정하는 영어 사용자 중심의 맞춤식 영어능력인증 시험제도입니다.
평가유형에 따른 개인별 장점과 단점을 파악하고, 개인별 영어학습 방향을 제시하는 성적분석자료를 제공하여
영어능력 종합검진 서비스를 제공함으로써 영어 사용자인 소비자와
영어능력 평가를 토대로 영어교육을 담당하는 교사 및 기관 인사관리자인 공급자를
모두 만족시키는 영어능력인증 평가입니다.

TOSEL은 인지적-학문적 언어 사용의 유창성 (Cognitive-Academic Language Proficiency, CALP)과
기본적-개인적 의사소통능력 (Basic Interpersonal Communication Skill, BICS)을
엄밀히 구분하여 수험자의 언어능력을 가장 친밀하게 평가하는 시험입니다.

대상	목적	용도
유아, 초, 중, 고등학생, 대학생 및 직장인 등 성인	한국인의 영어구사능력 증진과 비영어권 국가의 영어 사용자의 영어구사능력 증진	실질적인 영어구사능력 평가 + 입학전형 및 인재선발 등에 활용 및 직무역량별 인재 배치

연혁

2002.02	국제토셀위원회 창설 (수능출제위원역임 전국대학 영어전공교수진 중심)
2004.09	TOSEL 고려대학교 국제어학원 공동인증시험 실시
2006.04	EBS 한국교육방송공사 주관기관 참여
2006.05	민족사관고등학교 입학전형에 반영
2008.12	고려대학교 편입학시험 TOSEL 유형으로 대체
2009.01	서울시 공무원 근무평정에 TOSEL 점수 가산점 부여
2009.01	전국 대부분 외고, 자사고 입학전형에 TOSEL 반영 (한영외국어고등학교, 한일고등학교, 고양외국어고등학교, 과천외국어고등학교, 김포외국어고등학교, 명지외국어고등학교, 부산국제외국어고등학교, 부일외국어 고등학교, 성남외국어고등학교, 인천외국어고등학교, 전북외국어고등학교, 대전외국어고등학교, 청주외국어고등학교, 강원외국어고등학교, 전남외국어고등학교)
2009.12	청심국제중·고등학교 입학전형 TOSEL 반영
2009.12	한국외국어교육학회, 팬코리아영어교육학회, 한국음성학회, 한국응용언어학회 TOSEL 인증
2010.03	고려대학교, TOSEL 출제기관 및 공동 인증기관으로 참여
2010.07	경찰청 공무원 임용 TOSEL 성적 가산점 부여
2014.04	전국 200개 초등학교 단체 응시 실시
2017.03	중앙일보 주관기관 참여
2018.11	관공서, 대기업 등 100여 개 기관에서 TOSEL 반영
2019.06	미얀마 TOSEL 도입 발족식 베트남 TOSEL 도입 협약식
2019.11	2020학년도 고려대학교 편입학전형 반영
2020.04	국토교통부 국가자격시험 TOSEL 반영
2021.07	소방청 간부후보생 선발시험 TOSEL 반영

About TOSEL®

What's TOSEL?

"Test of Skills in the English Language"

TOSEL은 비영어권 국가의 영어 사용자를 대상으로 영어구사능력을 측정하여
그 결과를 공식 인증하는 영어능력인증 시험제도입니다.

영어 사용자 중심의 맞춤식 영어능력 인증 시험제도

맞춤식 평가

**획일적인 평가에서
세분화된 평가로의 전환**

TOSEL은 응시자의 연령별
인지단계에 따라 별도의 문항과 난이도를
적용하여 평가함으로써 평가의
목적과 용도에 적합한 평가 시스템을
구축하였습니다.

공정성과 신뢰성 확보

국제토셀위원회의 역할

TOSEL은 고려대학교가 출제 및 인증기관
으로 참여하였고 대학입학수학능력시험
출제위원 교수들이 중심이 된
국제토셀위원회가 주관하여
사회적 공정성과 신뢰성을 확보한
평가 제도입니다.

수입대체 효과

외화유출 차단 및 국위선양

TOSEL은 해외시험응시로 인한 외화의
유출을 막는 수입대체의 효과를 기대할 수
있습니다. TOSEL의 문항과 시험제도는
비영어권 국가에 수출하여 국위선양에
기여하고 있습니다.

Why TOSEL ® — 왜 TOSEL인가

01 학교 시험 폐지

일선 학교에서 중간, 기말고사 폐지로 인해 객관적인 영어 평가 제도의 부재가 우려됩니다. 그러나 전국단위로 연간 4번 시행되는 TOSEL 평가시험을 통해 학생들은 정확한 역량과 체계적인 학습방향을 꾸준히 진단받을 수 있습니다.

02 연령별/단계별 대비로 영어학습 점검

TOSEL은 응시자의 연령별 인지단계 및 영어 학습 단계에 따라 총 7단계로 구성되었습니다. 각 단계에 알맞은 문항유형과 난이도를 적용해 모든 연령 및 학습 과정에 맞추어 가장 효율적으로 영어실력을 평가할 수 있도록 개발된 영어시험입니다.

03 학교내신성적 향상

TOSEL은 학년별 교과과정과 연계하여 학교에서 배우는 내용을 학습하고 평가할 수 있도록 문항 및 주제를 구성하여 내신영어 향상을 위한 최적의 솔루션을 제공합니다.

04 수능대비 직결

유아, 초, 중등시절 어렵지 않고 즐겁게 학습해 온 영어이지만, 수능시험준비를 위해 접하는 영어의 문항 및 유형 난이도에 주춤하게 됩니다. 이를 대비하기 위해 TOSEL은 유아부터 성인까지 점진적인 학습을 통해 수능대비를 자연적으로 해나갈 수 있습니다.

05 진학과 취업에 대비한 필수 스펙관리

개인별 '학업성취기록부' 발급을 통해 영어학업성취이력을 꾸준히 기록한 영어학습 포트폴리오를 제공하여 영어학습 이력을 관리할 수 있습니다.

06 자기소개서에 토셀 기재

개별적인 진로 적성 Report를 제공하여 진로를 파악하고 자기소개서 작성시 적극적으로 활용할 수 있는 객관적인 자료를 제공합니다.

07 영어학습 동기부여

시험실시 후 응시자 모두에게 수여되는 인증서는 영어학습에 대한 자신감과 성취감을 고취시키고 동기를 부여합니다.

08 AI 분석 영어학습 솔루션

국내외 15,000여 개 학교·학원 단체 응시인원 중 엄선한 100만 명 이상의 실제 TOSEL 성적 데이터를 기반으로 영어인증시험 제도 중 세계 최초로 인공지능이 분석한 개인별 AI 정밀 진단 성적표를 제공합니다. 최첨단 AI 정밀진단 성적표는 최적의 영어 학습 솔루션을 제시하여 영어 학습에 소요되는 시간과 노력을 획기적으로 절감해줍니다.

09 명예의 전당, 우수협력기관 지정

우수교육기관은 'TOSEL 우수 협력 기관'에 지정되고, 각 시/도별, 최고득점자를 명예의 전당에 등재합니다.

Evaluation ——————— 평가

평가의 기본원칙

TOSEL은 PBT(Paper Based Test)를 통하여 간접평가와 직접평가를 모두 시행합니다.

TOSEL은 언어의 네 가지 요소인 **읽기, 듣기, 말하기, 쓰기 영역을 모두 평가합니다.**

문자언어

읽기능력

쓰기능력

음성언어

듣기능력

말하기능력

대한민국 대표 영어능력 인증 시험제도

TOSEL®

Reading 읽기	모든 레벨의 읽기 영역은 직접 평가 방식으로 측정합니다.
Listening 듣기	모든 레벨의 듣기 영역은 직접 평가 방식으로 측정합니다.
Writing 쓰기	모든 레벨의 쓰기 영역은 간접 평가 방식으로 측정합니다.
Speaking 말하기	모든 레벨의 말하기 영역은 간접 평가 방식으로 측정합니다.

TOSEL은 연령별 인지단계를 고려하여 **아래와 같이 7단계로 나누어 평가합니다.**

1 단계	**TOSEL**® COCOON	5~7세의 미취학 아동
2 단계	**TOSEL**® Pre-STARTER	초등학교 1~2학년
3 단계	**TOSEL**® STARTER	초등학교 3~4학년
4 단계	**TOSEL**® BASIC	초등학교 5~6학년
5 단계	**TOSEL**® JUNIOR	중학생
6 단계	**TOSEL**® HIGH JUNIOR	고등학생
7 단계	**TOSEL**® ADVANCED	대학생 및 성인

Grade Report —————— 성적표 및 인증서

개인 AI 정밀진단 성적표

십 수년간 전국단위 정기시험으로 축적된 빅데이터를 교육공학적으로 분석·활용하여 산출한 개인별 성적자료

정확한 영어능력진단 / 섹션별·파트별 영어능력 및 균형 진단 / 명예의 전당 등재 여부 / 온라인 최적화된 개인별 상세
성적자료를 위한 QR코드 / 응시지역, 동일학년, 전국에서의 학생의 위치

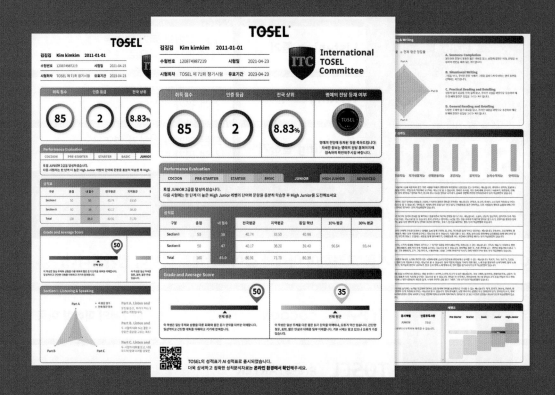

단체 및 기관 응시자 AI 통계 분석 자료

십 수년간 전국단위 정기시험으로 **축적된 빅데이터를
교육공학적으로 분석·활용**하여 산출한 응시자 통계 분석 자료

- 단체 내 레벨별 평균성적추이, LR평균 점수, 표준편차 파악
- 타 지역 내 다른 단체와의 점수 종합 비교 / 단체 내 레벨별
  학생분포 파악
- 동일 지역 내 다른 단체 레벨별 응시자의 평균 나이 비교
- 동일 지역 내 다른 단체 명예의 전당 등재 인원 수 비교
- 동일 지역 내 다른 단체 최고점자의 최고 점수 비교
- 동일 지역 내 다른 응시자들의 수 비교

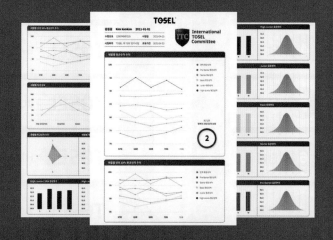

'토셀 명예의 전당' 등재

특별시, 광역시, 도 별 **1등 선발**
(7개시 9개도 **1등 선발**)

*홈페이지 로그인 - 시험결과 - 명예의 전당에서
해당자 등재 증명서 출력 가능

'학업성취기록부'에 토셀 인증등급 기재

개인별 **'학업성취기록부' 평생 발급**
진학과 취업을 대비한 **필수 스펙관리**

인증서

대한민국 초,중,고등학생의 영어숙달능력 평가 결과 공식인증

고려대학교 인증획득 (2010. 03)　팬코리아영어교육학회 인증획득 (2009. 10)　한국응용언어학회 인증획득 (2009. 11)

한국외국어교육학회 인증획득 (2009. 12)　한국음성학회 인증획득 (2009. 12)

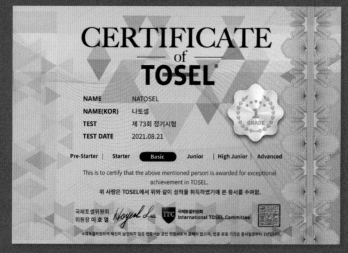

Grammar Series ——— 특장점

TOSEL 시험을 기준으로 빈출 지표를 활용한 문법 선정 및 예문과 문제 구성

TOSEL 시험 활용

☐ 실제 TOSEL 시험에 출제된 빈출 문항을 기준으로 단계별 학습을 위한 문법 선정

☐ 실제 TOSEL 시험에 활용된 문장을 사용하여 예문과 문제를 구성

☐ 문법 학습 이외에 TOSEL 기출 문제 풀이를 통해서 TOSEL 및 실전 영어 시험 대비 학습

세분화된 레벨링

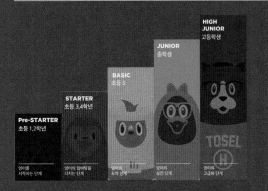

20년 간 대한민국 영어 평가 기관으로서

연간 4회 전국적으로 실시되는 정기시험에서

축적된 성적 데이터를 기반으로

정확하고 세분화된 레벨링을 통한

영어 학습 콘텐츠 개발

언어의 4대 영역 균형 학습 + 평가

1   TOSEL 평가: 학생의 영어 능력을 정확하게 평가

2   결과 분석 및 진단: 시험 점수와 결과를 분석하여 학생의 강점, 취약점,
     학습자 특성 등을 객관적으로 진단

3   학습 방향 제시: 객관적 진단 데이터를 기반으로 학습자 특성에 맞는
     학습 방향 제시 및 목표 설정

4   학습: 제시된 방향과 목표에 따라 학생에게 적합한 문법 학습법
     소개 및 영어의 체계와 구조 이해

5   학습 목표 달성: 학습 후 다시 평가를 통해 목표 달성 여부 확인 및
     성장을 위한 다음 학습 목표 설정

Grammar Series Level

TOSEL의 Grammar Series는 레벨에 맞게 단계적으로
문법을 학습할 수 있도록 구성되어 있습니다.

Pre-Starter	Starter	Basic	Junior	High Junior

- 그림을 활용하여 문법에 대한 이해도 향상
- 다양한 활동을 통해 문법 반복 학습 유도
- TOSEL 기출 문제 연습을 통한 실전 대비

- TOSEL 기출의 빈도수를 활용한 문법 선정으로 효율적 학습
- 실제 TOSEL 지문의 예문을 활용한 실용적 학습 제공
- TOSEL 기출 문제 연습을 통한 실전 대비

최신 수능 출제
문법을 포함하여
수능 대비 가능

70분 학습 Guideline

01 Unit Intro
2분

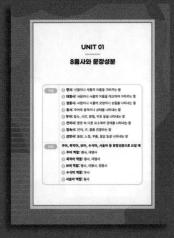

■ 중등 교육과정에서 익혀야 하는 문법을 중심으로
주요 개념별 학습 구성

■ 요약된 내용을 보고 단원의 개념에 대해 미리 생각해보기

02 개념
15분

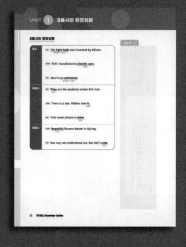

■ Unit Intro의 요약을 표로 구조화하여 세부적으로
학습하기 용이하게 구성

05 Error Recognition
8분

■ 수능 유형의 실전 문제 학습을 통해 TOSEL 시험 뿐만 아니라
수능 영어 또한 대비 가능

■ 5개년 TOSEL 기출을 활용하여 더욱 생생한 문법

06 Unit Review
10분

■ 빈칸을 채우는 형태로 구성하여 수업 시간 후
복습에 용이하게 구성

■ 배운 문법을 활용하여 예시 문장을 직접 써보는 시간

03
⏱ Exercise
10분

■ 다양한 Exercise 활동을 하며 혼동하기 쉬운
　문법 학습

■ 문장 안에 문법적으로 알맞은 단어를 선택하거나
　쓰는 활동을 하며 혼동하기 쉬운 문법 학습

04
✏ Sentence Completion
10분

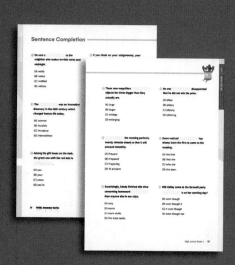

■ Unit에서 배운 문법을 활용하여 문제 해결하기

■ 빈칸 채우기, 알맞은 표현 고르기 등 TOSEL 실전 문제 학습

■ 틀린 문제에 대해서는 해당 Unit에서 복습하도록 지도하기

07
🔍 TOSEL 실전문제
15분

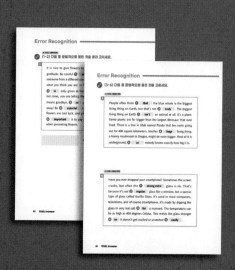

■ 실제 TOSEL 기출 문제를 통한 실전 대비 학습

■ 실제 시험 시간과 유사하게 풀이할 수 있도록 지도하기

■ 틀린 문제에 대해서는 해당 단원에서 복습하도록 지도하기

PreStarter/Starter/Basic Syllabus

PreStarter		Basic		2015 개정 초등 영어 언어형식
Chapter	Unit	Chapter	Unit	
I. 명사: 명사는 이름이야	1 셀 수 있는 명사	I. 명사	1 셀 수 있는 명사 앞에 붙는 관사 the/a/an	A boy/The **boy**/The (two) boys ran in the park. **The** store is closed.
	2 셀 수 있는 명사 앞에 붙는 관사 a/an		2 셀 수 없는 명사를 측정하는 단위	**Water** is very important for life. **Kate** is from **London**.
	3 셀 수 없는 명사		3 규칙 복수명사	
	4 명사의 복수형		4 불규칙 복수명사	The **two boys** ran in the park.
II. 대명사: 명사를 대신하는 대명사	1 주격 대명사	II. 대명사	1 단수대명사의 격	**She** is a teacher, and **he**'s a scientist. I like **your** glasses. What about **mine**?
	2 소유격 대명사		2 복수대명사의 격	**They**'re really delicious. **We** are very glad to hear from him.
	3 목적격 대명사		3 1, 2인칭 대명사의 활용	I like math, but Susan doesn't like it. He will help **you**.
	4 지시대명사		4 3인칭 대명사의 활용	Which do you like better, **this** or **that**? **These** are apples, and **those** are tomatoes. **That** dog is smart. **These/Those** books are really large.
III. 형용사: 명사&대명사를 꾸미는 형용사	1 형용사의 명사수식	III. 동사	1 동사의 기본시제	He **walks** to school every day. We **played** soccer yesterday. She **is going to** visit her grandparents next week. He **is sleeping** now. I **will visit** America next year.
	2 형용사의 대명사수식		2 동사의 불규칙 과거형	
	3 숫자와 시간		3 헷갈리기 쉬운 동사	**It's half past four**. **What time** is it?
				I **don't** like snakes. We **didn't** enjoy the movie very much.
	4 지시형용사		4 조동사	She **can** play the violin. Tom **won't** be at the meeting tomorrow. I **will** visit America next year. You **may** leave now.

Starter		Basic		2015 개정 초등 영어 언어형식
Chapter	Unit	Chapter	Unit	
I. 동사: 동사는 움직임이야	1 be동사	IV. 형용사와 부사	1 형용사 vs. 부사	**Many** young people have no money. We didn't buy **much/any** food. **Every** monkey likes bananas. **All** children love baby animals.
	2 의문사+be동사		2 수량형용사	
	3 3인칭 단수동사		3 빈도부사	We **usually** meet after lunch.
	4 동사의 현재시제		4 비교급과 최상급	Mary is **taller than I/me**.
II. 부사: 동사를 꾸미는 부사	1 일반적인 부사의 생김새	V. 접속사와 전치사	1 단어를 연결하는 접속사	John **and** Mary are good friends. They are my neighbors, **but** I don't know them well.
	2 예외적인 부사의 생김새		2 문장을 연결하는 접속사	He went to bed **because** he was sleepy.
	3 부사와 형용사의 비교		3 시간과 장소를 나타내는 전치사	There are two books **on** the desk.
	4 부사와 문장의 배열		4 그 밖의 전치사	
III. 전치사: 시간, 장소, 위치, 방향을 나타내는 전치사	1 시간을 나타내는 전치사	VI. 문장	1 문장의 형식	The baby **cried**. You **look happy** today. He **is a match teacher**. I **like** gimbap.
	2 장소를 나타내는 전치사		2 명령문	**Open** your book. **Let's go** to Brian's birthday party.
	3 위치를 나타내는 전치사		3 의문문	**Are you** ready? **Does** Anne work out on weekends?
	4 방향을 나타내는 전치사		4 부가의문문	**Why** did he leave early? **How** do you spell your name? **Who** can answer that question? **Whose dolls** are these? **What time** is it?

Junior Syllabus

Junior		2015 개정 중등 영어 언어형식
Chapter	**Unit**	
I. 8품사 (1)	1 명사	She lived in the **woods** when she was kid. Thank you for your **kindness**.
	2 대명사	I have **three books**. **One** is mine. **The others** are yours. **The chocolate cookie** is sweet. I'm going to have **another one**.
	3 형용사	Something **strange** happened last night.
	4 감탄사	**How** beautiful she is! **What** a player!
II 8품사 (2)	1 동사	Mathematics is my favorite subject. **Each** boy admires his teacher. **Both** the teacher **and** the students enjoyed the class. You can have **either** tea or coffee. It is **not only** beautiful **but (also)** useful.
	2 부사	
	3 전치사	
	4 접속사	I may stop by tomorrow **or** just phone you. Both the teacher **and** the students enjoyed the class.
III. 문장의 구조	1 문장성분의 기초	You can **put the dish on the table**. He **gave me a present**. They **elected him president**.
	2 문장의 형식	
	3 평서문의 전환	
	4 의문문의 비교	**Have you** finished your homework yet? This is your book, **isn't it**?
IV. 문장의 시제	1 단순시제	I **will be** able to help you get to the party tonight. **Are you going** to take the last train?
	2 진행시제	**I'm thinking** about the problem. I **was studying** when John called me.
	3 현재완료	The bakery **has been** open since 1960. He **has attended** the club meetings regularly.
	4 시간을 나타내는 접속사	**Since** he left this morning, I haven't seen him. **When** we arrived, she was talking on the phone.
V. to부정사와 동명사	1 to부정사	**To see** is **to belive**. Chris was glad **to hear the news**.
	2 동명사	We **enjoy swimming** in the pool. Life is **worth living**. I'm interested in **watching horror movies**.
	3 to부정사와 동명사 비교	
	4 의미상주어	It is difficult **for me to speak French**. It was kind **of you to help us**.
VI. 비교급과 최상급	1 비교급과 최상급의 규칙 변화	They've got **more/less** money **than** they need. A car is **much more** expensive **than** a motorbike.
	2 비교급과 최상급의 불규칙 변화	
	3 원급의 비교	You can run **as fast as** Billy can. She is old, but she is not **as old as** he (is).
	4 최상급의 비교	Cindy is **the shortest** of the three. It is **the most interesting** speech I've ever heard.

High Junior Syllabus

High Junior		2015 개정 중등 영어 언어형식
Chapter	**Unit**	
I. 문장의 형성	1 8품사와 문장 성분	The **audience** is/are enjoying the show. I'd like to **write a diary**, but I'm too busy to do so.
	2 문장의 형식	He**'s being** very rude. We **are hoping** you will be with us.
	3 문장의 배열	I think **(that)** he is a good actor. **Although/Though** it was cold, I went swimming.
	4 문장의 강조	The weather was **so** nice **that** we went hiking. **It was Justin who/that** told me the truth.
II 부정사와 동명사	1 원형부정사	You shouldn't **let** him **go** there again. I **heard** the children **sing/singing**.
	2 to부정사	He seemed **to have been ill (for some time)**. Bill promised Jane **to work out with her**. I remembered **John/John's coming late for class**. It goes without **saying that time is money**. There is no use **crying over the spilt milk**.
	3 동명사	
	4 to부정사와 동명사구	
III. 분사	1 현재분사	At the station I met a lady **carrying a large umbrella**. **With the night coming**, stars began to shine in the sky.
	2 과거분사	Wallets **found on the street** must be reported to the police.
	3 분사구문	**Walking along the street,** I met an old friend. **Having seen that movie before,** I wanted to see it again.
	4 독립분사구문	**Joshua returning home,** the puppy ran toward him. **Frankly speaking,** I failed the test.
IV. 수동태	1 수동태의 형성	The building **was built** in 1880. I **was made** to clean the room. Nolan **was seen** to enter the building. The monkey **has been raised** by human parents for years. Cooper **will be invited** to today's meeting. The information superhighway **will have been introduced** to everyone by 2015.
	2 수동태와 능동태의 전환	
	3 수동태와 전치사의 사용	
	4 주의해야 할 수동태 용법	
V. 관계대명사와 관계부사	1 관계대명사의 사용	The girl **who is playing the piano** is called Ann. This is the book **(that) I bought yesterday**.
	2 관계대명사와 선행사	Please tell me **what happened**.
	3 관계대명사의 생략	This is **why** we have to study English grammar.
	4 관계부사	The town **in which I was born** is very small. That's just **how he talks**, always serious about his work.
VI. 가정법	1 가정법 현재와 과거	**If it were not for you,** I **would** be lonely.
	2 가정법 과거완료	**Had** I had enough money, I **would have bought** a cell phone. **Without/But for** your advice, I **would have** failed.
	3 혼합가정법	I **wish** I **had learned** swimming last summer. He acts **as if** he **had been** there.
	4 특수가정법	I'd **rather** we **had** dinner now. **Provided that/As long as** they had plenty to eat, the crew **seemed** to be happy.

CHAPTER 4

Ⅳ. 수동태

UNIT 01 수동태의 형성   **21**

UNIT 02 수동태와 능동태의 전환   **31**

UNIT 03 수동태와 전치사의 사용   **41**

UNIT 04 주의해야 할 수동태 용법   **51**

TOSEL 실전문제 4   **61**

UNIT 01

수동태의 형성

개념	주어가 수동적으로 동작을 당할 때 사용하는 동사의 형태
생김새	**be+p.p** ex) My coffee <u>was **spilled**</u> by her.
쓰임	**❶ 동작의 행위자에 초점을 두지 않을 때** ex) Dorothy <u>was **invited**</u> to this party by Eugene. **❷ 수동태의 주어가 문맥상 분명할 때** ex) The robber <u>was **arrested**</u> last night by them. **❸ 동일한 주어를 쓰려는 구문상의 필요가 있을 때** ex) She had great results and <u>was **promoted**</u>. **❹ 감정·피해·종사·출생 등을 나타낼 때** ex) I <u>am **interested**</u> in studying foreign languages.

수동태가 사용되는 경우

능동태: 주어가 동작을 능동적으로 행하는 것
수동태: 주어가 동작을 수동직으로 당하는 것

> **❶ 동작의 행위자가 불분명할 때**
>
> George <u>was wounded</u> in the war.
>   be + p.p
>
> **❷ 수동태의 주어가 문맥상 분명할 때**
>
> Donald Jones <u>was elected</u> president.
>   be + p.p
>
> **❸ 행위자를 밝히고 싶지 않을 때**
>
> Things that shouldn't have been spoken <u>have been said</u>.
>   have been+p.p
>
> **❹ 능동태의 주어보다는 수동태의 주어에 더 관심이 있을 때**
>
> The child <u>was run over</u> by a car.
>   be + p.p

NOTE ✐

❺ 동일한 주어를 쓰려는 구문상의 필요가 있을 때

He made a speech and <u>was asked</u> many questions in the end.
                         be + p.p

❻ 감정·피해·종사·출생 등을 나타낼 때

감정   I <u>was pleased</u> to receive a present.
        be + p.p

피해   The ship <u>was wrecked</u> in the storm.
              be + p.p

종사   He <u>is engaged</u> in foreign trade.
         be + p.p

출생   Elvis Presley <u>was born</u> in 1935.
             be + p.p

NOTE

Exercise

 Exercise 1

둘 중 맞는 단어를 골라 문장을 완성하세요.

❶ His invention was recognizing / recognized by the people.

❷ They were disappointing / disappointed with the news.

❸ The deer was ate / was eaten by the tiger.

❹ He found / was found the bag she wished to buy.

❺ None of them asked / was asked a question by the police officer.

 Exercise 2

주어진 단어들을 바르게 배열해 문장을 완성하세요.

❶ 그 종이는 찢어졌다.

➜ _____.

(torn, paper, was, the)

❷ 그 아이스크림은 초콜릿으로 덮여 있다.

➜ _____.

(is, chocolate, the ice cream, covered, with)

❸ Ella가 입고 있는 옷은 Bill에 의해 만들어졌다.

➜ _____.

(by Bill, Ella, the cloth, is, is, wearing, made)

 Exercise 3

주어진 표현을 활용하여 빈칸을 채워 문장을 완성하세요.

---

1 Lee _____ by the guard yesterday. (be catch)

2 The umbrella _____ . (be break)

3 Her aunt _____ in environmental research. (be engage)

4 Wilson and his twin brother _____ in 2005. (be bear)

5 The students _____ by their teachers. (be call)

6 Science _____ a great study. (is consider)

Sentence Completion

1 Was anybody .... in the car accident?

(A) injure

(B) injures

(C) injured

(D) had injured

2 I am completely .... by this artwork. I'd like to learn more about it.

(A) intrigue

(B) intrigues

(C) intrigued

(D) intriguing

3 One of Jen's best friends .... nominated for a prize.

(A) be

(B) was

(C) may

(D) were

4 This elderly gentleman may .... some help with his bags.

(A) need

(B) needed

(C) be need

(D) be have need

5 The shadow that had frightened the children was actually the birdhouse that .... on the tree next door.

(A) was hung

(B) was hang

(C) was hangs

(D) was hanged

6 Those stories .... by the famous Australian writer.

(A) was create

(B) was created

(C) were created

(D) were creating

7 When they came home, the drain pipe _____ due to cold weather.

(A) freeze

(B) frozen

(C) freezing

(D) was frozen

8 The graduation party will _____ this weekend. The students are excited.

(A) held

(B) be held

(C) was held

(D) were held

9 Whenever you want, you can _____ me for my help.

(A) call

(B) calls

(C) called

(D) is called

10 10 years ago, she _____ as one of the most beautiful women in the world.

(A) knows

(B) known

(C) is known

(D) was known

11 The microwave _____ to her by her older brother when she moved to this house.

(A) is given

(B) was given

(C) were given

(D) having given

12 That photo which _____ by Sam contains memories of his school days.

(A) taken

(B) taking

(C) is taken

(D) was taken

Error Recognition

● TOSEL 기출문제 변형 수능/내신 출제유형

틀린 문장 고르기

다음 중 문법적으로 <u>틀린</u> 것을 고르세요.

> Mason has a pet hamster named Hampton. Hampton has light brown and white fur and adorable pink paws. Mason is a writer, and he ❶ **stays** up late at night. Hampton also stays up late at night. His busiest times are at sunrise and sunset. At those times, he ❷ **loves** to run around and around in a plastic ball outside of his cage, near Mason. He also likes to hide in an ❸ **empty** toilet paper roll. The rest of the time, he runs on a wheel in his cage for exercise. For treats, he enjoys ❹ **eating** seeds, especially sunflower seeds. A whole bunch is ❺ **take** by him all at once and stores them in the big pouches of his cheeks. Then his cheeks get big and puffy.

고쳐쓰기

틀린 문장의 번호를 쓰고 올바르게 고치세요.

⟶ _____

● TOSEL 기출문제 변형 수능/내신 출제유형

틀린 문장 고르기

다음 중 문법적으로 <u>틀린</u> 것을 고르세요.

Franz Reichelt was an Austrian-French tailor. He died **①** **doing** something very dangerous. He had designed a kind of parachute suit for pilots. He wanted to test it. He used a doll to test it by **②** **throwing** it off the fifth floor of a building. However, Reichelt thought he needed a higher place for it to be **③** **testing** . He chose the Eiffel Tower in Paris. Reichelt got permission from the Paris police to do the test. On February 4, 1912, Reichelt prepared the parachute on the first level of the tower. However, he had no doll. He was **④** **going** to put the parachute on himself! The police and other observers tried to stop him. However, Reichelt **⑤** **wanted** to prove it could work for other humans. He jumped. Sadly, the test was a failure. The parachute did not open. Reichelt fell 57 meters to the ground and died.

고쳐쓰기

틀린 문장의 번호를 쓰고 올바르게 고치세요.

배운 내용 스스로 정리해보기

수동태의 형성

수동태는 ❶ [   ] 이(가) 불분명할 때, ❷ [   ] 이(가) 문맥상 분명할 때,

❸ [   ] 을(를) 밝히고 싶지 않을 때, ❹ 수동태의 주어에 더 관심이 있을 때,

❺ [   ] 을(를) 쓰려는 구문 상의 필요가 있을 때, ❻ [   ] 등을 나타낼 때 사용된다.

예시문장 써보기

❶ 동작의 행위자가 불분명할 때

➜ _____

❷ 수동태의 주어가 문맥상 분명할 때

➜ _____

❸ 행위자를 밝히고 싶지 않을 때

➜ _____

❹ 수동태의 주어에 더 관심이 있을 때

➜ _____

❺ 동일한 주어 쓰려는 구문상의 필요가 있을 때

➜ _____

❻ 감정·피해·종사·출생 등을 나타낼 때

감정 ➜ _____

피해 ➜ _____

종사 ➜ _____

출생 ➜ _____

UNIT 02

수동태와 능동태의 전환

생김새	**'S + V + O ~'** → **'S + be V + p.p. + ~ + by 목적격'** ex) The dog chased the cat. → The cat was chased by the dog.
쓰임	**목적어가 있는 능동태 문장을** **같은 의미의 수동태 문장으로 전환할 때** ❶ **3형식**: 'S(O) + beV + p.p + by 목적격' ❷ **4형식**: 'S(I.O) + beV + p.p + O(D.O) + by 목적격', 'S(D.O) + beV + p.p + (전치사) + O(I.O) + by 목적격' ❸ **5형식**: 'S(O) + beV +p.p + S.C(O.C) + by 목적격'

UNIT 2 수동태와 능동태의 전환

❶ 3~5형식 수동태의 전환

3형식

He respected his uncle.
주어　　동사　　　목적어

→ His uncle was respected by him.
목적어 → 주어　　　동사(beV + p.p)　주어 → by + 목적격

4형식

He gave his friend a pen.
주어　동사　　간접목적어　직접목적어

→ His friend was given a pen (by him).
간접목적어 → 주어　동사(beV + p.p) 직접목적어 → 목적어

→ A pen was given (to) his friend (by him).
직접목적어 → 주어 동사(beV + p.p) 간접목적어 → (to) + 목적격

5형식

They elected him chairman.
주어　　동사　　목적어　　목적격보어

→ He was elected chairman (by them).
목적어 → 주어 동사(beV + p.p) 목적격보어 → 주격보어

→ Chairman was elected him (by them). (X)
목적어가 아니므로 수동태의 주어가 될 수 없음.

NOTE

TIP 4형식 문장의 전환

- 의미상 어색한 경우, 직접목적어 혹은 간접목적어 중 하나만 수동태의 주어로 사용 가능함.

- He bought her a bunch of flowers.
→ A bunch of flowers was bought for her by him.
→ She was bought a bunch of flowers by him. (X)

- He envied me my success.
→ I was envied my success by him.
→ My success was envied me by him. (X)

TIP 수동태를 취할 수 없는 동사

단어	뜻
resemble	닮다
suit	맞다
become	어울리다
possess	가지다
cost	소요되다
lack	부족하다
let	허락하다
have	가지다
befall	닥치다

② 문형에 따른 수동태의 전환

의문문

Who invented this machine?
주격   동사   목적어

→ By whom was this machine invented?
   by + 목적격 beV 주어   p.p

Whom do you love?
목적격 do 주어 동사

→ Who is loved by you?
   주격 be V + p.p by + 목적격

Is he writing a new book?
beV 주어 동사   목적어

→ Is a new book being written by him?
   beV   주어   beV + p.p   by + 목적격

명령문

Do it at once.
동사 목적어

→ Let it be done at once.
   사역동사 주어 be + p.p

Don't touch the bag.
   동사   목적어

→ Don't let the bag be touched. 동사 let 부정
   사역동사   주어   be + p.p

→ Let the bag not be touched. 원형부정사 be 부정
   사역동사 주어   not be + p.p

Exercise

 ## Exercise 1

둘 중 맞는 단어를 골라 문장을 완성하세요.

❶ He   resembles / is resembled   his grandfather.

❷   Let / Lets   it be sent to your teacher until tomorrow.

❸ That man   witnesses / was witnessed   yesterday at the park.

❹   Who / By whom   was this cake delivered?

❺ Ben   was given / had given   a cup of milk for his breakfast.

 ## Exercise 2

주어진 문장을 능동태로 바꾸세요.

❶ The rabbit was caught by the lion.

➡ _____.

❷ Susan was given a birthday present by Jack.

➡ _____.

❸ Although his name was Jihoon, he was called Charlie by his parents.

➡ Although his name was Jihoon, _____.

 Exercise 3

주어진 문장을 수동태로 바꾸세요.

① I love chocolate flavored marshmallows.

➜ _____.

② You borrowed books from the school library.

➜ _____ from the school library.

③ The manager praised the player for his character.

➜ _____ for his character.

④ Everyone in our class calls her the genius.

➜ _____.

⑤ The rich man buys the little child a teddy bear.

➜ _____.

⑥ Nick gives his wife a ring.

➜ _____.

➜ _____.

Sentence Completion

1 The wooden chest, which was
_____ to Maria by her
grandmother, sat in the dining room.

(A) give

(B) gave

(C) given

(D) giving

2 I _____ some coconut crackers
that my friend sent from Africa.

(A) have

(B) having

(C) was had

(D) was have

3 She _____ by her older sister
to live selfishly, rather than being a fool.

(A) recommend

(B) recommended

(C) was recommend

(D) was recommended

4 The watch she received from her parents
_____ as much as 1,000 dollars.

(A) cost

(B) costs

(C) was cost

(D) were cost

5 When people play computer games, they
unintentionally _____ their real
personality.

(A) reveal

(B) revealed

(C) revealing

(D) was revealed

6 The song she made _____ for its
mysterious melody and lyrics.

(A) known

(B) knowing

(C) was known

(D) was knowing

7 Who _____ by the students is not certain yet, but it will be announced this afternoon.

(A) elects

(B) elected

(C) is elected

(D) is electing

8 _____ was the piano played last week? I was so busy that I couldn't watch the performance.

(A) Who

(B) Whom

(C) Whose

(D) By whom

9 Is the washing machine _____ by someone else now? I must use it immediately.

(A) use

(B) used

(C) been used

(D) being used

10 _____ the chemicals be touched without safety equipment since it is very dangerous to do so.

(A) Let

(B) Do let

(C) Let not

(D) Don't let

11 Let the mirror on the wall _____ until further instructions are given.

(A) was moved

(B) be moved not

(C) not be moved

(D) wasn't moved

12 Let the room _____ regularly. It isn't good for your health to leave it dirty.

(A) clean

(B) cleaned

(C) be cleaned

(D) was cleaned

Error Recognition

 틀린 문장 고르기

다음 중 문법적으로 <u>틀린</u> 것을 고르세요.

> What color is the universe? Two scientists at a university ① **wanted** to find the answer to this question. The research ② **was revealed** some interesting information. At the beginning of their research, the scientists thought that the average color of the universe was greenish-white. However, they later discovered the universe was actually beige. The two scientists wrote a correction about the color. They ③ **published** it in a magazine for other scientists. Then, they asked the magazine's readers to name the color. The readers ④ **voted** on the suggestions. One popular choice was "univeige." Despite the popularity of "univeige," the two researchers ⑤ **liked** a different name. That name was "cosmic latte." Now, "cosmic latte" is the official term for the average color of the universe.

 고쳐쓰기

틀린 문장의 번호를 쓰고 올바르게 고치세요.

● TOSEL 기출문제 변형 수능/내신 출제유형

틀린 문장 고르기

다음 중 문법적으로 <u>틀린</u> 것을 고르세요.

Metal is so important to humans that world time periods have even been ① **described** accordingly by the metal used: the Bronze Age and the Iron Age. However, many of the metals in use today are not pure metals, but rather alloys, also known as metallic compounds. These are metals that ② **combine** at least two elements. They are harder and stronger than pure metal alone. One particularly strong type of alloy is steel, which comes in various types. A common type of steel includes iron ③ **combined** with small amounts of carbon. Another kind of alloy is aluminum. Aluminum combined with elements like copper and silicon is strong, yet light. A third alloy is solder, which ④ **made** out of lead and tin. Solder is used to put other pieces of metal together. Its range of use ⑤ **extends** from plumbing, to electronics, to jewelry.

고쳐쓰기

틀린 문장의 번호를 쓰고 올바르게 고치세요.

배운 내용 스스로 정리해보기

① 3~5형식 수동태의 전환

'S + V + O + ~' 형태의 능동태 문장을   형태의 수동태 문장으로 전환할 수 있다.

능동태 문장을 수동태 문장으로 전환하기

❶ They canceled the schedule.

➜ _____

❷ She sent me the document.

➜ _____

❸ We call her a genius.

➜ _____

② 문형에 따른 수동태의 전환

❶   와(과) **❷**   등도 수동태로 전환될 수 있다.

능동태 문장을 수동태 문장으로 전환하기

❶ Who explained this phenomenon?

➜ _____

❷ Memorize all the manuals.

➜ _____

UNIT 03

수동태와 전치사의 사용

생김새	**'S + beV + p.p + ~ + 전치사 + 목적격'** ex) I <u>was shocked</u> <u>at</u> the news.

쓰임	**수동태와 함께 쓰이는 '전치사+목적격'이 숙어처럼 사용될 때**
	
	❶ by
	   ex) The solution was found <u>by</u> them.
	
	❷ to
	   ex) Asher was married <u>to</u> Bonita last year.
	
	❸ at
	   ex) He was disappointed <u>at</u> getting the lowest score.

다양한 전치사를 쓰는 수동태

수동태 동사와 함께 전치사 by가 일반적으로 사용되지만,
이외에 다른 전치사들도 사용된다.

by	The remote controller <u>was found</u> <u>by</u> her. 　　　　　　　　　beV + p.p　　by + 목적격 The concert <u>was canceled</u> <u>by</u> the bad weather. 　　　　　　beV + p.p　　　　　　　by + 목적격 He <u>is known</u> <u>by</u> his father. 　　beV + p.p　　by + 목적격
to	He <u>is known</u> <u>to</u> everybody. 　　beV + p.p　　to + 목적격 It <u>is known</u> that friends are important (<u>to</u> people). 　beV + p.p　　　　　　　　　　　　　　　to + 목적격
at	Alice <u>was surprised</u> <u>at</u> the news. 　　　beV + p.p　　　at + 목적격 The children <u>were marveled</u> <u>at</u> the cartoon. 　　　　　beV + p.p　　　at + 목적격
in	Martha <u>was immersed</u> <u>in</u> finding the answer. 　　　　beV + p.p　　　in + 목적격 They <u>were disappointed</u> <u>in</u> his absence. 　　　beV + p.p　　　in + 목적격 I <u>am interested</u> <u>in</u> jazz music. 　beV + p.p　　in + 목적격

for	He is known for his novels. beV + p.p　　for + 목적격 Vladivostok is known for crabs. beV + p.p　　for + 목적격 This restaurant is known for its excellent cuisine. beV + p.p　　for + 목적격
with	I am satisfied with my score. beV + p.p　　with + 목적격 She was delighted with her son's letter. beV + p.p　　with + 목적격 The road is covered with snow. beV + p.p　　with + 목적격
about	My grandparents were worried about my trip. beV + p.p　　about + 목적격 They were worried about their future plan. beV + p.p　　about + 목적격

Exercise

 ## Exercise 1
둘 중 맞는 단어를 골라 문장을 완성하세요.

❶ She was not satisfied   with / by   the result.

❷ This idol group is known   as / to   K-pop fans all over the world.

❸ Ted was surprised   to / at   the news that they were getting married.

❹ My mother is known   as / for   her special cookie recipe.

❺ Kevin was worried   with / about   his grandfather's health.

 ## Exercise 2
주어진 단어들을 바르게 배열해 문장을 완성하세요.

❶ Susan은 그녀의 시험 점수에 대해 걱정했다.

➜ _____ .

(worried, Susan, her test score, was, about)

❷ Bob은 새들이 나는 것을 보는 데에 완전히 몰두되어 있었다.

➜ _____ .

(birds, in, was, fly, immersed, totally, watching, Bob)

❸ 실종된 소년을 경찰이 찾았다.

➜ _____ .

(was, the missing boy, by, found, the police)

 Exercise 3

주어진 표현을 사용하여 빈칸을 채워 문장을 완성하세요.

❶ My boss _____ the sales report that I gave yesterday.
(be satisfy)

❷ This electronic device _____ its good quality at a reasonable price. (be know)

❸ People _____ the news of his sudden death. (be surprise)

❹ Kristen _____ my Christmas gift. (be delight)

❺ The festival _____ government order last week.
(be cancel)

❻ Neil _____ his son's recent behavior.(be worry)

Sentence Completion

1 He didn't answer her call because he was not satisfied ⬚⬚⬚ her late reply.

(A) to

(B) by

(C) for

(D) with

2 He was completely ⬚⬚⬚ at the news, so he couldn't close his mouth.

(A) found

(B) known

(C) surprised

(D) immersed

3 Some people were worried ⬚⬚⬚ economic crisis when the UK decided to leave the EU.

(A) to

(B) by

(C) with

(D) about

4 Some critics say she is over the hill, but she is still known ⬚⬚⬚ her powerful acting skill.

(A) to

(B) at

(C) for

(D) with

5 Gina was so disappointed ⬚⬚⬚ the decision her daughter made, but she still loved her.

(A) in

(B) to

(C) as

(D) within

6 I was born in Salzburg which is ⬚⬚⬚ for salt.

(A) known

(B) satisfied

(C) canceled

(D) delighted

7 When we went to the beach, we were marveled ⬚⬚⬚ sea turtles laying eggs in the sand.

(A) by

(B) to

(C) at

(D) for

8 As the saying goes, one is known ⬚⬚⬚ the company one keeps. You should choose a good friend.

(A) for

(B) by

(C) to

(D) in

9 My coworkers are mostly ⬚⬚⬚ their working environment.

(A) found by

(B) known to

(C) canceled by

(D) satisfied with

10 Evan is always ⬚⬚⬚ his son. His son wants to be a soldier and he is now in a military academy.

(A) known to

(B) immersed in

(C) worried about

(D) disappointed in

11 Tony was immersed ⬚⬚⬚ building a model train station.

(A) for

(B) in

(C) by

(D) to

12 The West End Musical <Matilda> is known ⬚⬚⬚ its catchy songs and interesting story.

(A) to

(B) for

(C) with

(D) during

Error Recognition

● TOSEL 기출문제 변형 수능/내신 출제유형

 틀린 문장 고르기

다음 중 문법적으로 <u>틀린</u> 것을 고르세요.

I like to collect model rocket ships. My favorite one is my Saturn V rocket ship that my friend ❶ **gave** me. It was very expensive. It cost over 150 dollars! I keep the model in my room on my desk. It is about 1 meter long, but the real Saturn V rocket ship was about 100 times longer. I put the model together by myself, and it took a long time. I spent 15 hours ❷ **gluing** the 2,000 plastic pieces. When I finished, I ❸ **was pleased** the perfectly completed work. The white and black rocket ship is very shiny and beautiful. Now, I always show guests my Saturn V rocket ship model when they ❹ **come** to my house. One day, I want ❺ **to make** an even bigger model, maybe one that is over 2 meters long!

 고쳐쓰기

틀린 문장의 번호를 쓰고 올바르게 고치세요.

● TOSEL 기출문제 변형 수능/내신 출제유형

틀린 문장 고르기

다음 중 문법적으로 <u>틀린</u> 것을 고르세요.

When people get sick they often take some medicine to relieve pain. However, sometimes patients receive pills or shots with no real medicine in them. Such a pill or shot ❶ **is known to** a "placebo." If someone's feelings of pain change due to a placebo, we call this the "placebo effect." The placebo effect does not usually ❷ **last** a long time. However, it can still help people ❸ **to feel** some relief for a little while. But it can also make people feel worse. When a placebo effect is negative, it ❹ **is called** a "nocebo effect." How can sick people feel better or worse from pills with no real medicine? The answer is about beliefs. If a person believes and expects ❺ **that** a pill has an effect, the person's feelings of pain can sometimes change. Researchers think the human body can create chemicals that change feelings of pain.

고쳐쓰기

틀린 문장의 번호를 쓰고 올바르게 고치세요.

 배운 내용 스스로 정리해보기

다양한 전치사를 쓰는 수동태

수동태 동사와 함께 전치사 ❶   가 일반적으로 사용되지만,

이외에 다른 전치사들도 사용된다. 다른 전치사들은 ❷   , ❸   ,

❹   , ❺   , ❻   , ❼   이(가) 있다.

예시문장 써보기

❶ by → _____

❷ to → _____

❸ at → _____

❹ in → _____

❺ for → _____

❻ with → _____

❼ about → _____

UNIT 04

주의해야 할 수동태 용법

| 쓰임 | **3~5형식 문장의 수동태 용법 이외에**
문장의 구성에 따라 수동태의 형태가 달라진다.

ex) I looked after her.

→ She was looked after by me.

ex) You should wear a woolen hat.

→ A woolen hat should be worn by you.

ex) Nobody can pronounce this word.

→ This word cannot be pronounced by anybody. |

❶ 목적어가 절인 경우

They say that he is honest.
　주어　동사　　　목적어

➡ It is said that he is honest (by them).
　가주어 beV + p.p　　목적어 → 진주어　　주어 → by + 목적격

➡ He is said to be honest (by them).
　주어　beV + p.p　　to부정사　　주어 → by + 목적격

➡ That he is honest is said. (X) that절은 수동태의 주어가 될 수 없음.

❷ 동사구의 수동태

❶ 자동사 + 전치사

Everybody laughed at him.
　　주어　　　　동사　전치사 + 목적격

➡ He was laughed at by everybody.
　주어　beV + p.p　전치사　주어 → by + 목적격

❷ 자동사 + 부사 + 전치사

They looked up to him.
　주어　　동사　부사 전치사 + 목적격

➡ He was looked up to by them.
　주어　beV + p.p　부사 전치사 주어 → by + 목적격

❸ 타동사 + 명사 + 전치사

We should take care of the orphan.
　주어　　동사　　명사　　전치사 + 목적격

➡ The orphan should be taken care of.
　　주어　　　beV + p.p　명사 전치사

➡ Care should be taken of the orphan.
　명사　　beV + p.p　　전치사 + 목적격

❸ 조동사가 있는 수동태

You must solve the problem.
　주어　조동사 + 동사원형　　목적어

➡ The problem must be solved by you.
　목적어 → 주어　　조동사 + be + p.p　주어 → by + 목적격

NOTE 🖉

TIP **완료형 부정사의 사용**

• 주절의 동사보다 that절의 동사가 앞선 시제일 때 완료형 부정사를 씀.

• They say that he was a teacher.

➡ He is said to have been a teacher.

---

④ 부정문의 수동태

Nobody can solve this problem.
주어　　조동사 + 동사원형　　목적어

→ This problem **cannot be solved** by anybody.
　목적어 → 주어　　조동사 + not + be + p.p　　주어 → by + 목적격

→ This problem **can be solved** by nobody. (X)

⑤ 지각·사역동사의 수동태

We saw her enter the room.
주어　지각동사 목적어　　목적격보어

→ She was seen to enter the room.
목적어 → 주어　beV + p.p　　　to부정사

We made him go.
주어　사역동사　목적어 목적격보어

→ He was made to go.
목적어 → 주어　beV + p.p　to부정사

⑥ 동작·상태 수동태

❶ 동작 수동태

He **get**s accustom**ed** to living here.
주어　get [become, grow] + p.p

❷ 상태 수동태

The treasure **lie**s hidden in the cave.
　　주어　　lie [stand, remain, rest] + p.p

❸ 태의 전환시제

We paint our house every year.
주어　동사　　목적어

→ Our house is paint**ed** every year.
　목적어 → 주어　beV + p.p

NOTE

TIP Anybody와 Nobody

● 능동태에서 'Anybody cannot solve this problem.'은 틀린 형태 이므로, 'Nobody can solve this problem'으로 써야 함.

TIP 사역동사 have와 let

● 사역동사 have와 let은 수동태로 쓰일 수 없으므로 각각 'be asked to'와 'be allowed to'의 형태로 쓰임.

Exercise

Exercise 1

둘 중 맞는 단어를 골라 문장을 완성하세요.

❶ My grandmother was   taken care of by / taken care by of   uncle Bob.

❷ The man is said   that / to be   a son of the former president.

❸ Eugene was made   to leave / leave   the castle by the royal guards.

❹ That monster cannot be killed by   nobody / anybody   .

❺ The body of Pharaoh lies   hiding / hidden   in Egyptian pyramids.

Exercise 2

주어진 단어들을 바르게 배열해 문장을 완성하세요.

❶ 그 왕은 그의 백성에 의해 존경받았다.

➔ _____ .

(people, the, to, king, his, up, by, was, looked)

❷ Tina가 아침에 조깅하는 것이 보였다.

➔ _____ .

(the, seen, in, to, was, morning, Tina, jog)

❸ 모든 전자기기는 영화 상영 전에 꺼져야한다.

➔ _____ .

(turned, before, electronic devices, starts, be, the movie, off, should, all)

 Exercise 3

주어진 표현을 활용하여 빈칸을 채워 문장을 완성하세요.

① The suspect _____ enter his neighbor's house at midnight.
(be see)

② Thomas _____ hearing train sound when sleeping.
(get accustom)

③ Organic chemistry _____ be one of the most difficult subjects
in college. (be say)

④ More than 250 dogs and cats _____ this animal shelter.
(be take care of)

⑤ He lay _____ under the sand after a sandstorm. (bury)

⑥ The students were _____ with anything. (not satisfy)

Sentence Completion

1 It is said ⬚⬚⬚⬚⬚ the former king was killed by poison.

(A) what
(B) that
(C) to be
(D) which

2 Do you see that guy? He is said ⬚⬚⬚⬚⬚ a CEO of a big IT corporation.

(A) to
(B) that
(C) what
(D) to be

3 A little kitten is taken ⬚⬚⬚⬚⬚ its mother.

(A) care by
(B) care by of
(C) by care of
(D) care of by

4 The man wearing a ridiculous hat was ⬚⬚⬚⬚⬚ by his colleagues.

(A) laughed at
(B) looked up to
(C) taken care of
(D) satisfied with

5 The sword will ⬚⬚⬚⬚⬚ by the future ruler of England.

(A) pull
(B) is pulled
(C) was pulle
(D) be pulled

6 Required documentations should ⬚⬚⬚⬚⬚ by tomorrow.

(A) is submitted
(B) be submitted
(C) was submitted
(D) was submitted

7 This maze cannot be escaped by

.

(A) anybody

(B) nobody

(C) somebody

(D) everybody

10 He was made   smoking cigarettes by his doctor.

(A) quit

(B) quits

(C) to quit

(D) quitting

8 She was not forced to end a relationship

with him by   .

(A) no one

(B) nobody

(C) anybody

(D) everybody

11 At last the truth about the tragic accident

            known to us.

(A) lay

(B) stood

(C) became

(D) remained

9 Barbara was seen   the homeless in a soup kitchen last week.

(A) help

(B) helped

(C) helping

(D) to help

12 It is said that the gate of that white castle on the hill   locked for more than 100 years.

(A) got

(B) grew

(C) became

(D) remained

Error Recognition

 틀린 문장 고르기

다음 중 문법적으로 <u>틀린</u> 것을 고르세요.

One of the most fascinating human body parts is our hair. The more scientists study the hair on the human head, the more interesting facts they have discovered. One interesting aspect is how ❶ **many** hairs we have. There ❷ **are** up to 150,000 of them on each person's head! Moreover, we lose about 50 hairs a day, and each hair ❸ **was only lasted** about four years. Therefore, we carry around thousands of new hairs in our lifetime. Another unique aspect of hair that scientists ❹ **have been researching** is its strength. One single strand of hair can hold up to 100g in weight. While hair is not as strong as steel, it is about as strong as the material used in bullet-proof vests. Researchers are now looking into ways hair can ❺ **be used** in armor.

 고쳐쓰기

틀린 문장의 번호를 쓰고 올바르게 고치세요.

➡ _____

● TOSEL 기출문제 변형 수능/내신 출제유형

틀린 문장 고르기

다음 중 문법적으로 <u>틀린</u> 것을 고르세요.

The Lyubov Orlova was a Russian ship with a mysterious ending. It was very sturdy and could sail in icy waters. It went to very cold places both the Arctic and the Antarctic. But then one day the company in charge of the ship had some problems with payments. The ship ❶ **was taken away from** its owners. For two years, it stayed near Newfoundland in Canada. Later the ship was going to ❷ **pull apart** . A small but powerful boat ❸ **was brought in** to take the ship away. However, while the Lyubov Orlova ❹ **was being pulled** away in the sea near Canada, the rope snapped. The small boat could not control the big ship, and the Lyubov Orlova floated away. It ❺ **left** Canadian waters and went into international waters. The Canadian government said it was not their problem, and the ship simply floated around. In the end, it probably sank. But no one really knows where the Lyubov Orlova went.

고쳐쓰기

틀린 문장의 번호를 쓰고 올바르게 고치세요.

 _____

Unit Review

✏️ 배운 내용 스스로 정리해보기

① 목적어가 절인 경우

예시문장 써보기

가주어 It을 사용 → _____

② 동사구의 수동태

예시문장 써보기

'자동사 + 부사 + 전치사'의 수동태 문장 → _____

③ 조동사가 있는 수동태

능동태 문장을 수동태 문장으로 전환하기

'They should fix the printer.' → _____

④ 부정문의 수동태

능동태 문장을 수동태 문장으로 전환하기

'Nobody would notice the change.' → _____

⑤ 지각·사역동사의 수동태

예시문장 써보기

❶ 지각동사의 수동태 문장 → _____

❷ 사역동사의 수동태 문장 → _____

⑥ 동사구의 수동태

예시문장 써보기

동작 수동태 문장 → _____

TOSEL 실전문제 ④

PART 6. Sentence Completion

DIRECTIONS: In this portion of the test, you will be given 12 incomplete sentences. From the choices provided, choose the word or words that correctly complete the sentence. Then, fill in the corresponding space on your answer sheet.

1. Many students are concerned _____ their future, and what they want to do in the future.

    (A) at
    (B) on
    (C) for
    (D) about

2. These three history books written by Dr. Lynn _____ mainly in the class.

    (A) used
    (B) will use
    (C) are used
    (D) to be used

3. When we reached the train station, we found that all the trains _____ due to heavy snowfall.

    (A) delay
    (B) be delayed
    (C) were delaying
    (D) were delayed

4. My younger sister _____ with the products delivered because it was not exactly what she requested.

    (A) disappoints
    (B) was disappointing
    (C) was disappointed
    (D) has disappointed

5. Yoga was developed by the Indus-Sarasvati civilization in India, and has _____ for over 5,000 years.

    (A) exist
    (B) exists
    (C) existed
    (D) been existed

6. Could you speak up a little because people at the back can't hear what is _____?

    (A) saying
    (B) to say
    (C) been said
    (D) being said

7. Diego is a famous soccer star playing for BB Barcelona, and also known _____ his work as a children's rights activist.

(A) by
(B) at
(C) for
(D) with

8. The renovated parking garage is _____ under Mr. Romano's uptown office building.

(A) locate
(B) located
(C) locating
(D) been located

9. The private key is only shared with the key's generator and must _____ with a password.

(A) protects
(B) protecting
(C) be protected
(D) have protected

10. It _____ one in every seven residents of San Francisco works in a technical services sector.

(A) is said that
(B) is said to be
(C) is saying what
(D) is saying to be

11. They always get together and speak quietly not to be overheard by _____ in class.

(A) nobody
(B) no one
(C) everyone
(D) anybody

12. We are made _____ diverse activities such as debate, acting or project study in the literature class.

(A) do
(B) did
(C) to do
(D) done

TOSEL 실전 문제

Error Recognition

(1~2) 다음 중 문법적으로 틀린 것을 골라 고치세요.

1

Ladies and Gentlemen, welcome to Adventure World, the most
❶ exciting place on Earth! The crocodile show will **❷ be held**
three times today, at 2:00, 3:00, and 4:30. The fire dancers can
be **❸ seen** at 1:00 and 2:30. Sadly, the knife-throwing show
❹ has canceled due to an accident. We **❺ hope** you enjoy
your time here at Adventure World!

 ➡ _____

2

Victoria Hansen is a world-famous opera singer. She has given concerts all over America and Europe and **❶ is well known to** her high, beautiful voice. Some of her best roles **❷ are** Miss Mona in The Best House in Texas, and Mrs. Peachum in The Three Penny Opera. This year, she will **❸ star** in Bon Appétit, a musical about cooking. Mrs. Hansen has also performed a set of songs called "Deep Spaces" **❹ written** especially for her by Stephen Scott, her husband. Not **❺ touring** the globe, she is a professor of music at Colorado College.

➡ _____

Error Recognition

3

On the first day in May, my hometown **❶ holds** a May Day festival. Every year, one local girl **❷ is choosing** to be the May Queen. She marches in the parade, and **❸ wears** a white dress and flowers. After that, there is Morris dancing, for which we wear bells on our legs. Finally, we all tie **❹ colorful** ribbons around a Maypole **❺ in** the town center.

4

Saffron is a very unique spice. It **❶ comes** from the crocus, a purple flower from the iris family. Each flower has only three stigmas, thin strands in the flower's center. These must **❷ carefully picked** by hand and then dried. **❸ Harvesting** saffron takes a lot of work. This is why saffron is so expensive. In fact, saffron is the most expensive spice in the world. Fortunately, only a little saffron **❹ is needed** to add its bright yellow color and special flavor to foods. While mainly used in cooking today, saffron was once **❺ used** in medicines and perfumes as well.

5

It all began with a newspaper ad with a picture of Santa saying, "Call me on my private phone, and I will ① **talk** to you personally." But the number ② **was printed** wrong. It was actually the number for Colonel Harry Shoup at the Continental Air Defense Command center, now known as NORAD. So on Christmas Eve of 1955, Colonel Shoup began ③ **receiving** calls from kids wanting to speak with Santa. He didn't want to disappoint them. So he said that he ④ **was tracking** Santa's sleigh by radar. And so the NORAD Santa Tracker ⑤ **born** .

6

Annapurna refers to a mountain range in the Himalayas of Nepal. Its name ① **means** "full of food" or "goddess of harvest." This mountain range consists of six major peaks that are over 7000 meters tall. One of its peaks, Annapurna I, ② **is known for** being extremely dangerous among mountain climbers. Climbers who have died trying to reach its summit ③ **including** Russian Anatoli Boukreev in 1997 and Korean Park Young-seok in 2011. Fortunately for most people, Annapurna may ④ **be experienced** from a safer point. Around the Annapurna range is a popular trek ⑤ **called** the Annapurna Circuit. It takes about 20 days to complete.

수능 대비 문제

CHAPTER 5

Ⅴ. 관계대명사와 관계부사

UNIT 01 관계대명사의 사용   69

UNIT 02 관계대명사와 선행사   79

UNIT 03 관계대명사의 생략   89

UNIT 04 관계부사   99

TOSEL 실전문제 5   109

UNIT 01

관계대명사의 사용

생김새	**who, which, that, whom, whose, of which, what** ex) I saw the woman <u>**who**</u> waited here.

쓰임	**❶ 주격관계대명사**
	
	    ex) I met <u>a boy</u>. + **He** wore a long coat.
	
	    ➜ I met <u>a boy</u> <u>**who**</u> wore a long coat.
	
	❷ 소유격관계대명사
	
	    ex) I bought <u>this bag</u>. + **Its** color is white.
	
	    ➜ I bought <u>this bag</u> <u>**whose**</u> color is white.
	
	❸ 목적격관계대명사
	
	    ex) This is <u>the house</u>. + We want to buy **the house**.
	
	    ➜ This is <u>the house</u> **that** we want to buy.

❶ 선행사와 격변화

격 \ 선행사	사람	사물	사람 · 사물	선행사 포함
주격	who	which	that	what
소유격	whose	whose, of which	-	-
목적격	whom	which	that	what

The man **who** employed me would transport anything.
　선행사　주격관계대명사

She has a daughter **whose** name is Nancy.
　　　선행사　　　소유격관계대명사

He met distant relatives (**whom**) he had never seen.
　　　선행사　　　목적격관계대명사

NOTE ✎

TIP 관계대명사의 기능
● '접속사+대명사'의 기능을 함.

TIP 목적격관계대명사
● 목적격관계대명사는 생략 가능함.

❷ 관계대명사 which

❶ 선행사가 사물 · 동물

I have many shells (**which**) she has collected. 목적격
= I have many shells. + She has collected many shells.

Look at the house **whose** roof(=**of which** the roof) is red. 소유격
= Look at the house. + The house's roof is red.

❷ 선행사가 앞 문장의 일부 또는 전체 (계속적 용법에서만 사용 가능)

He wants to go to Guam, **which** is impossible. 문장 일부
= He wants to go to Guam. + To go to Guam is impossible.

I said nothing, **which** made her angry. 문장 전체
= I said nothing. + She was angry because I said nothing.

❸ 선행사가 형용사 · 동사

He is rich, **which** she is not. 형용사
= He is rich. + She is not rich.

Alex cleaned my room, **which** he did often. 동사
= Alex cleaned my room. + Alex often cleaned my room.

❸ 관계대명사 that

관계대명사 that은 항상 한정적[제한적] 용법으로 쓴다.

> The table **that[which]** stands in the corner is mine.
> <u>선행사</u>   주격관계대명사
>
> = The table stands in the corner. + The table is mine.
>   주격

➜ **관계대명사 that만 사용하는 경우**

  ❶ 한정적 의미가 부각된 경우

> • She is <u>the only person</u> **that** I met yesterday.
>
> • He spent <u>all the money</u> **that** he had earned.
>
> • Which is <u>the car</u> **that** you want to buy?

  ❷ 관계사절의 동사가 be동사, 관계대명사가 보어인 경우

> • My air conditioner is not the machine that it was.

➜ **관계대명사 that을 사용하지 않는 경우**

  선행사에 부정관사가 있어 한정의 의미가 약한 경우

> • Sara is <u>a woman</u> **whom** he likes.
>   선행사   목적격관계대명사
>
> ➜ Sara is <u>a woman</u> **that** he likes. (X)

➜ **관계대명사 that과 전치사**

  관계대명사 that 앞에, 전치사 사용 불가

> • He is <u>the very man</u> **that** I have been looking <u>for</u>.
>   선행사   목적격관계대명사
>
> ➜ He is <u>the very man</u> <u>for</u> **that** I have been looking. (X)

NOTE

Exercise

 ## Exercise 1

둘 중 맞는 단어를 골라 문장을 완성하세요.

① Jessica is the first student who / which graduated from this school.

② That is the car whom / which I wished to buy.

③ Don't hesitate to learn from the man whose / whom idea is creative.

④ Peter is the man who / whom Stella loves.

⑤ For the ones who / whose desire to succeed, she will give a lecture.

 ## Exercise 2

주어진 단어들을 바르게 배열해 문장을 완성하세요.

① 나는 기절하기 직전이었던 소년을 구했다.

→ _____.

(about to faint, was, I, the boy, saved, who)

② 너는 그가 가져온 그 컴퓨터를 사용해도 된다.

→ _____.

(he brought, you, the computer, can, which, use)

③ Noa는 짧은 머리를 가진 작은 소녀다.

→ _____.

(is, a little girl, is, Noa, whose, hair, short)

 Exercise 3

주어진 문장들을 한 문장으로 바꾸세요. (단, that 사용 불가)

① They are friends. They knew each other for 10 years.

➜ _____.

② He has a ring. The ring is bold.

➜ _____.

③ She wants to visit her teacher. Her teacher has big eyes.

➜ _____.

④ Olive met a strong man. She fell in love with him.

➜ _____.

⑤ Chris is handsome. Fredrick is not handsome.

➜ _____.

⑥ He is wearing a hat. The hat is blue.

➜ _____.

Sentence Completion

1. Ray and Judy, _____ met at a party, have been married fifty years.

    (A) who
    (B) which
    (C) whom
    (D) whose

2. Do you know that girl in Grade 7 _____ gave a speech about racism?

    (A) she
    (B) her
    (C) who
    (D) whose

3. She was a famous writer _____ everyone loved for more than 100 years.

    (A) who
    (B) which
    (C) whom
    (D) whose

4. Don't let the dog break the vase _____ pattern is drawn by Alex.

    (A) that
    (B) who
    (C) whom
    (D) whose

5. The scarf _____ he gave to his grandmother helped to find her when she was lost.

    (A) who
    (B) which
    (C) whom
    (D) whose

6. This is the book _____ Grace tried to get, but eventually she never had a chance to read it.

    (A) who
    (B) which
    (C) whom
    (D) whose

7 If you don't mind, I would like to use this cup _____ handle is big.

(A) that

(B) which

(C) whom

(D) whose

10 People used to believe _____ the world was flat and not a sphere.

(A) that

(B) which

(C) whom

(D) whose

8 They are dancing in a circle, _____ is a kind of a ritual they do annually.

(A) that

(B) which

(C) whom

(D) whose

11 Confused by his message, Yuri decided to ask the only person _____ is responsible for this matter.

(A) that

(B) what

(C) whom

(D) whose

9 She was the strongest woman _____ I had ever seen.

(A) why

(B) that

(C) what

(D) there

12 The one she is holding is the perfect suit _____ Dave was looking for.

(A) it

(B) she

(C) that

(D) for that

Error Recognition

 틀린 문장 고르기

다음 중 문법적으로 <u>틀린</u> 것을 고르세요.

Jenna loves ❶ **her** scooter. Jenna has bad balance, so she likes its two small, sturdy front wheels and a big wheel in the back. They are very stable. Also, they have a bumpy surface, which keeps her from falling off. To control the scooter, Jenna just needs to lean to each side. However, her mother doesn't allow her to ride it to school. She thinks ❷ **that** it is dangerous. Moreover, she thinks that students ❸ **who** ride their scooters to school have bad attitudes. Jenna doesn't agree with her. Jenna told her mother that those students ❹ **whose** her mother thinks have bad attitudes are in fact excellent students. Those ❺ **who** study hard and listen well to their teachers can also ride their scooters to school. What is more, since she always wears her helmet, it is not as dangerous as her mother thinks it is.

 고쳐쓰기

틀린 문장의 번호를 쓰고 올바르게 고치세요.

_____

● TOSEL 기출문제 변형 수능/내신 출제유형

 ## 틀린 문장 고르기

다음 중 문법적으로 <u>틀린</u> 것을 고르세요.

Last week Davina, Joseph, and their dad went out to see a baseball game. They were very excited because this was the first time they all went out together to see a sports game. Davina and Joseph were looking forward to seeing their favorite baseball players ① playing right in front of them. But on the way there, Davina and Joseph had an argument about where to sit. Joseph wanted to sit with fans of the Marlins ② which he liked - but Davina wanted to sit with fans of the Tigers which she liked. Although they both liked baseball, they did not root for the same team. Their dad asked them to meet each other halfway so ③ that they could watch the game together. However, they did not give an inch. They argued for an hour, but could not reach the solution with ④ that they both can be satisfied. In the end, their dad made a decision. He did not even like baseball, so they all went to a basketball game ⑤ which is his favorite.

 ## 고쳐쓰기

틀린 문장의 번호를 쓰고 올바르게 고치세요.

 배운 내용 스스로 정리해보기

❶ 수동태의 형성

격\선행사	사람	사물	사람·사물	선행사 포함
주격	❶	❹	that	what
소유격	❷	whose, ❺	-	-
목적격	❸	❻	that	what

예시문장 써보기

사람을 가리키는 목적격관계대명사 ➡ _____

❷ 관계대명사 which

관계대명사 which는 선행사가 사물·동물, _____, 그리고 형용사·동사인 경우에 쓴다.

예시문장 써보기

선행사가 앞 문장의 일부 또는 전체

➡ _____

❸ 관계대명사 that

관계대명사 that은 항상 _____ 용법으로 쓴다.

예시문장 써보기

한정적[제한적] 용법

➡ _____

UNIT 02

관계대명사와 선행사

생김새	**what, 전치사+which, 관용표현 등** ex) This is **<u>what</u>** I have chosen.
쓰임	**선행사를 포함한 관계대명사 what** ① **명사절 이끄는 경우** 　ex) The cook made me **<u>what</u>** I wanted. ② **관계형용사로 쓰이는 경우** 　ex) Give me **<u>what</u>** <u>alternative</u> you have. ③ **관용용법** 　ex) She is **<u>what</u>** <u>people call</u> a genius violinist.

❶ 관계대명사 what

관계대명사 what은 선행사를 포함한다.

❶ 명사절을 이끄는 경우

My father made me **what** I am now.
= My father made me **the man that** I am now.

You will be sorry for **what** you have done.
= You will be sorry for **the thing which** you have done.

I will give you **what** you want to have.
= I will give you **all that** you want to have.

❷ 관계형용사로 쓰이는 경우

I gave him **what** money I had.
= I gave him **all** the money **that** I had.

I gave him **what** little money I had.
= I gave him **all the little money that** I had.

→ 관용용법

what one is (사람의 상태)	He is not **what** he was. = He is not the man **that** he was. = He is not **what** he used to be.
what one has (사람의 재산)	Do not judge a man by **what** he has. = Do not judge a man by the thing **that** he has.
A is to B **what C is to D** (A와 B의 관계는 C와 D의 관계와 같다)	Reading is to the mind **what** food is to the body. = As food is to the body, so is reading to the mind.
What is +비교급/최상급 (더욱/가장 ~한 것은)	He is clever, and **what** is **better**, very brave. I lost my way, and **what** is **worst**, it is raining.
What A call (소위 말하는)	He is **what** people **call** a medical specialist.

❷ 관계대명사의 두 가지 용법

제한적 용법	He had a son **who** became a doctor.
계속적 용법	He had a son, **who** became a doctor.

➡ **관계대명사 that과 계속적 용법**

- I like the boy, **that** is honest and diligent. (X)
  계속적 용법에서는 관계대명사 that을 쓸 수 없음

  ⇨ I like the boy, **who** is honest and diligent. (O)

❸ 관계대명사와 전치사의 용법

This is <u>the book</u>. + I am searching <u>for</u> <u>the book</u>.

➡ This is the book <u>for</u> **which** I am searching.
  관계대명사 앞에 전치사가 위치함

= This is the book **(which)** I am searching <u>for</u>.
  관계대명사와 떨어져 전치사가 문장의 맨 끝에 위치함

➡ **전치사가 반드시 관계대명사 앞에 위치해야 하는 경우**

  ❶ 한정어구

- I have many books, <u>some of which</u> are expensive.

  ❷ 전치사의 관계부사화

- Monday is the day **on which** we are busiest.
= Monday is the day **when** we are busiest.

➡ **전치사가 관계대명사 앞에 올 수 없는 경우: 관용어구**

- It was the very thing <u>**(that)**</u> I <u>was afraid</u> <u>of</u>.

- Drawing is an amusement <u>**(which)**</u> I <u>am</u> particularly <u>fond</u> <u>of</u>.

NOTE

UNIT 2 관계대명사와 선행사

Exercise

 ## Exercise 1

둘 중 맞는 단어를 골라 문장을 완성하세요.

① I know   which / what   you want.

② Go and see   which / what   they are preparing for.

③ Jiyoung has two friends,   who / what   are athletes.

④ Joseph remembers   which / what   he did last night.

⑤ We know three students,   who / that   received high scores.

 ## Exercise 2

주어진 단어들을 바르게 배열해 문장을 완성하세요.

① Bob은 그 남자에게 쫓기고 있었는데, 그는 무서운 얼굴을 하고 있었다.

→ _____.

(was being, by the man, Bob, who, chased, a scary face, had)

② 너는 무엇이 먼저 마무리되어야 하는지 안다.

→ _____.

(should, you, what, be done, know, first)

③ 그 영화의 주제는 내가 무서워하는 것이다.

→ _____.

(of, the one, the movie's topic, afraid, is, that, I am)

 Exercise 3

주어진 문장을 선행사가 있는 문장으로 바꾸세요.

---

❶ This is what she asked me to do.

➜ _____.

❷ Julia is not what she dreamed to be.

➜ _____.

❸ What you said cannot be true.

➜ _____.

❹ People tend to judge others with what one has.

➜ _____.

❺ Don't let them take what you deserve to get.

➜ _____.

❻ What Ilay gave his teacher is his essay.

➜ _____.

Sentence Completion

① Ella remembers _____ she and her grandmother promised when she was young.

(A) why

(B) that

(C) what

(D) there

② Those who think they are always right sometimes ignore _____ others say.

(A) that

(B) what

(C) whom

(D) whose

③ The jacket on the couch is _____ I bought yesterday for you.

(A) it

(B) me

(C) that

(D) what

④ This candle smells good, and _____ is better, this warms the room.

(A) that

(B) what

(C) where

(D) the thing

⑤ That's _____ people try their best to get the favor of others, but sometimes fail.

(A) the time that

(B) the thing that

(C) the thing which

(D) the reason why

⑥ He and I watched two action movies, _____ he waited for the release of.

(A) that

(B) what

(C) which

(D) where

7 We met two boys, [_____] helped us find our daughter at the amusement park yesterday.

(A) who
(B) what
(C) whom
(D) whose

8 Austin met Alice, [_____] he spent his childhood. They used to hang out together.

(A) who
(B) whom
(C) of whom
(D) with whom

9 Do you know that man, [_____] hat is purple and glasses are black?

(A) whom
(B) whose
(C) in whom
(D) of whose

10 This smartphone is the one [_____] he was looking for. I should buy one.

(A) that
(B) what
(C) to which
(D) for which

11 Mike repaired 20 cars, some of [_____] were so old that no one than him could fix them.

(A) it
(B) which
(C) theirs
(D) what

12 Nobody expected him to leave this company [_____] he worked so hard.

(A) what
(B) which
(C) in which
(D) for what

Error Recognition

 틀린 문장 고르기

다음 중 문법적으로 <u>틀린</u> 것을 고르세요.

Do you ever feel like you are just running from one activity to another? In school, do you rush from one subject to another? When things happen at such a fast pace, you should stop yourself every now and then to think about ❶ **that** you've been doing or learning. Self-reflection means slowing down and calming yourself. By being calm and ❷ **going** slowly, you give your brain a chance to evaluate the input it has already received. You can do these in your mind or keep a journal of written notes. Whether written or purely mental, the process is the same. Look for the times when you complete a unit of study in the subjects you are learning. Think and write down some notes on the new things ❸ **that** you learned. Let your mind think about the notes ❹ **that** you have written and make some connections. Also, think about things ❺ **that** you are unsure of. This will help you remember to look for answers the next time you are working with the same topic.

 고쳐쓰기

틀린 문장의 번호를 쓰고 올바르게 고치세요.

⬛⬛⬛⬛⬛ ➡ _____

● TOSEL 기출문제 변형 수능/내신 출제유형

 ## 틀린 문장 고르기

다음 중 문법적으로 <u>틀린</u> 것을 고르세요.

Most people can only sing one note at a time, but in Mongolia, there is a special type of singing ❶ **called** Khoomei. People ❷ **who** use this technique can sing two or more notes at once! Singers make a low note ❸ **using** their throat, and they use their tongue, lips, and jaw, to make higher notes. Men have traditionally sung this way at festivals and workplaces while more and more woman performers have started to learn and ❹ **practice** Khoomei. Now, there are many singers in Mongolia, ❺ **that** travel around the world to introduce the beauty of this traditional singing technique.

 ## 고쳐쓰기

틀린 문장의 번호를 쓰고 올바르게 고치세요.

✏️ 배운 내용 스스로 정리해보기

① 관계대명사 what

관계대명사 what은 ❶ _____ 을(를) 포함하며 ❷ _____ 에 사용된다.

예시문장 써보기

❶ 명사절을 이끄는 목적격 관계대명사 ➜ _____

❷ 관용용법(관계 의미) ➜ _____

② 관계대명사의 두 가지 용법

관계대명사는 선행사를 의미상 제한해주는 ❶ _____ 와(과)

선행사의 추가적 의미를 계속해서 서술해주는 ❷ _____ 이 있다.

예시문장 써보기

❶ 제한적 용법 ➜ _____

❷ 계속적 용법 ➜ _____

③ 관계대명사와 전치사의 용법

전치사의 목적어를 대신하는 관계대명사는 ❶ _____ 에 해당 전치사를 붙이거나

❷ _____ 에 남겨둔다.

예시문장 써보기

❶ which 앞에 전치사 위치 ➜ _____

❷ 문장 맨 끝에 전치사 남겨두기 ➜ _____

UNIT 03

관계대명사의 생략

개념	관계대명사는 생략되거나 변형된 형태로 사용될 수 있음
생략	**❶ 목적격** ex) The meeting **(that)** we rescheduled was canceled. **❷ 선행사 표시** ex) I miss the day **(on which / when / that)** we played the piano together. **❸ 주격 + beV** ex) The agenda **(which was)** covered last time was important.

❶ 관계대명사의 생략

목적격	**It was all he could <u>do</u> to prevent the danger.** = It was all <u>that</u> he could <u>do</u> to prevent the danger. 　　　　동사 do의 목적어 **The house I live <u>in</u> is located in the suburbs.** = The house <u>which</u> I live <u>in</u> is located in the suburbs. 　　　　전치사 in의 목적어 **I have two spare rooms, <u>neither of</u> <u>which</u> I used.** = We have two spare rooms, <u>neither of</u> we used. (X) 　　　　　전치사(구)
선행사 표시	**Tell me the day he will arrive.** = Tell me the day <u>on which</u> he will arrive. = Tell me the day <u>when</u> he will arrive. = Tell me the day <u>that</u> he will arrive. **That is the reason he left.** = That is the reason <u>for which</u> he left. = That is the reason <u>why</u> he left. = That is the reason <u>that</u> he left.
주격 + beV	**The number of people attending was big.** = The number of people <u>who</u> <u>were</u> attending was big. **The problem, discussed, was insolvable.** = The problem, <u>which</u> <u>was</u> discussed, was insolvable.

NOTE ✎

TIP 전치사 + 목적격관계대명사

● 전치사 + 목적격관계대명사 일 때는 관계대명사의 생략이 불가능하다. 단, 전치사가 목적격관계대명사가 이끄는 문미에 있을 때는 관계대명사를 생략할 수 있다.

② 유사 [의사] 관계대명사

as	He entertained as many guests **as** came to the party. 주격관계대명사 Take as much **as** you want. 목적격관계대명사
but	He is not such a fool **but** can see the truth. 주격관계대명사(that+not) He is not such a fool **but** he can know the truth. 접속사
than	He has more money **than** you have. 목적격관계대명사(비교의 의미) I know you better **than** (I know) her. 접속사

③ 복합관계대명사

모든, 어떠한	명사적 용법 I will give it to **whoever** comes first. = I will give it to anyone who comes first. I will give it to **whomever** I like. = I will give it to anyone whom I like. 형용사적 용법 You may take **whichever** course you want. = You may take any course which you want.
양보	**Whomever** you invite, I don't mind. = No matter whom you invite, I don't mind. **Whichever** you take, you cannot be satisfied. = No matter which you take, you cannot be satisfied. **Whatever** you may say, I shall go there. = No matter what you may say, I shall go there.

NOTE

Exercise

 ## Exercise 1

둘 중 맞는 단어를 골라 문장을 완성하세요.

1 They are not the students whose / that I taught.

2 Editors who / X working here are writing books.

3 She is not so silly who / but can bake some delicious bread.

4 Just go and meet who / whoever comes into your mind.

5 That is the person who / X preparing this food.

 ## Exercise 2

주어진 단어들을 바르게 배열해 문장을 완성하세요.

1 네가 원하는 것을 무엇이든지 나에게 말해라.

→ _____ .

   (you, me, want, Tell, anything)

2 이것이 네가 예약한 자리가 맞니?

→ _____ .

   (reserved, this, the right, Is, you, seat)

3 나는 누구든지 이기는 사람에게 이 돈을 줄 것이다.

→ _____ .

   (wins, will, I, this money, to, give, whoever)

 Exercise 3

적절한 관계대명사를 사용하여 빈칸을 채워 문장을 완성하세요.

---

① James married Lica, _____ is a dentist.

② If you don't mind, let Nancy call her parents _____ she loves.

③ Is this the bag _____ you gave him?

④ I wish I could buy this car _____ has big wheels.

⑤ I forgot to bring the file _____ includes his resume.

⑥ _____ you choose, you will be satisfied with it.

Sentence Completion

1 It will be hard for the brown bear to endure the hot weather ⬚⬚⬚ he never experienced before.

(A) that

(B) who

(C) whom

(D) where

2 Many people don't exactly know what happened to the boy ⬚⬚⬚ was adopted by Peter.

(A) X

(B) he

(C) who

(D) whom

3 Do you know the physicist ⬚⬚⬚ received the Nobel Prize?

(A) X

(B) who

(C) whom

(D) which

4 This Sunday, Minha will go to the church ⬚⬚⬚ she spent her school days at.

(A) who

(B) which

(C) whom

(D) the place

5 The guitar player, ⬚⬚⬚ also a famous dancer, will appear on the show tonight.

(A) who

(B) which

(C) whom

(D) who is

6 Please let me know when you would like to visit her, ⬚⬚⬚ you could get some help from.

(A) who

(B) which

(C) whom

(D) whose

7 Our neighbors eat more eggs

＿＿＿＿＿ we do, so we sometimes
share our eggs with them.

(A) as

(B) but

(C) than

(D) that

10 ＿＿＿＿＿ you work with, you
should respect your colleagues.

(A) Whoever

(B) No matter

(C) No matter who

(D) No matter whom

8 As a history expert, he taught as many

students ＿＿＿＿＿ study history.

(A) as

(B) but

(C) than

(D) which

11 According to Sally's husband, she will

invite ＿＿＿＿＿ is willing to come
to the party.

(A) who

(B) whom

(C) anyone who

(D) anyone whom

9 It is certain that Ruby will love

＿＿＿＿＿ gift you give, so don't
worry.

(A) who

(B) which

(C) whoever

(D) whichever

12 No matter ＿＿＿＿＿ Kevin thinks,
I will not believe him because he is a liar.

(A) who

(B) what

(C) whoever

(D) whatever

Error Recognition

 틀린 문장 고르기

다음 중 문법적으로 <u>틀린</u> 것을 고르세요.

Diamonds are generally thought of ❶ **as** precious and valuable stones that are pricey due to their extreme rarity, but this is not necessarily true. How exactly did the diamonds become so expensive? Two hundred years ago, diamonds were truly rare and were mostly owned by royalty while commoners had ❷ **little** interest in them. Then, a very large deposit of diamonds was discovered in South Africa, making them common and cheap. At this point, a single company gradually started ❸ **to buy and control** all of the diamonds, creating a monopoly. This company then manipulatd the amount of diamonds on the market and used advertisements to artificially drive up their price and make people ❹ **think** diamonds had more value ❺ **but** other jewels had. This led to the idea that diamonds should be expensive and are needed for special occasions such as weddings.

 고쳐쓰기

틀린 문장의 번호를 쓰고 올바르게 고치세요.

● TOSEL 기출문제 변형 수능/내신 출제유형

 틀린 문장 고르기

다음 중 문법적으로 <u>틀린</u> 것을 고르세요.

> An archeologist is a person who studies human history by digging up and examining historical sites and artifacts. You might not think that finding an old toilet would be exciting but, for an archeologist, it is a fantastic discovery. This kind of discovery can be very helpful for learning about a certain time period due to the waste **①** **stored** in them. Recently, an outhouse (an old style of toilet) that is believed to be from the year 1711 has been excavated. This is especially **②** **exciting** because people from that time period were known to use their outhouses not only for relieving themselves, but also throwing away their household trash. **③** **Whomever** this trash is, scientists can learn about the historical people's lifestyle habits, and **④** **what** they ate. Their household trash can also be analyzed to reveal **⑤** **what** everyday life was like for such people.

 고쳐쓰기

틀린 문장의 번호를 쓰고 올바르게 고치세요.

[   ]   ➔   _____

Unit Review

✏️ 배운 내용 스스로 정리해보기

❶ 관계대명사의 생략

예시문장 써보기

❶ 목적격 관계대명사의 생략 → _____

❷ 주격 + beV의 생략 → _____

❷ 유사 [의사] 관계대명사

유사 [의사] 관계대명사에는 ❶ _____, ❷ _____, ❸ than이 있다.

예시문장 써보기

❶ as → _____

❷ than → _____

❸ 복합관계대명사

복합관계대명사는 ❶ _____, ❷ _____ 의 의미를 가진다.

예시문장 써보기

❶ 모든 어떠한의 의미 → _____

❷ 양보의 의미 → _____

UNIT 04

―――

관계부사

종류	**when, where, why, how, that** ex) This is <u>the bookstore</u> **where** I work.
쓰임	**관계부사는 '접속사+부사'의 역할을 하며** **각각 시간, 장소, 이유, 방법을 나타내는 선행사 뒤에 위치함**
생략	**관계부사와 또는 그의 선행사는 조건부로 생략될 수 있음** ex) I remember <u>(the day)</u> **when** we first met. ex) I know <u>the reason</u> **(why)** he didn't attend the class.

① 종류와 용법

선행사	관계부사	전치사 + 관계대명사	용법
시간	when	at[on, in] which	제한적 · 계속적
장소	where	at[on, in, to] which	제한적 · 계속적
이유	why	for which	제한적
방법	how	in which	제한적
시간 · 장소 · 이유 · 방법	that	at[on, in, to, for] which	제한적

NOTE ✎

TIP 관계대명사 vs 관계부사

● 관계대명사 + 불완전한 문장
● 관계부사 + 완전한 문장

when

I don't know the day **when** he will come back.
제한적 용법
= I don't know the day on which he will come back.
전치사 + 관계대명사

Wait till Saturday, **when** I will let you know.
계속적 용법
= Wait till Saturday, and then I will let you know.

where

This is the town **where** I was born.
제한적 용법
= This is the town in which I was born.
전치사 + 관계대명사

They came to us, **where** they lodged a night.
계속적 용법
= They came to us, and there they lodged a night.

why

Tell me the reason **why** you were absent.
제한적 용법
= Tell me the reason for which you were absent.
전치사 + 관계대명사

how

This is **how** it happened.
제한적 용법(선행사 생략)
= This is the way **that** it happened.
관계부사
= This is the way in which it happened.
전치사 + 관계대명사
= This is **the way** it happened.
선행사(how생략)
≠ This is **the way how** it happened. (X)

TIP the way와 how

● the way와 how는 같은 의미의 부사이므로 함께 쓸 수 없다. 둘 중 하나는 반드시 생략해야 함.

❷ 관계부사의 생략

Is that <u>the reason</u> <u>**(why)**</u> you didn't come?
      선행사   관계부사

<u>The exact time</u> <u>**(when)**</u> he did it is not known.
   선행사   관계부사

She got married on <u>the day</u> <u>**(when)**</u> John arrived.
               선행사   관계부사

❸ 선행사의 생략

This is <u>(the place)</u> **where** I once lived.
        선행사   관계부사

This is <u>the very house</u> **where** I once lived.
   선행사(특정장소이므로 생략 불가능) 관계부사

I want to go <u>(to the place)</u> **where** you are going.
          선행사   관계부사

❹ 복합관계부사

'관계부사 + ever'형태이며, why는 복합관계부사로 쓰지 않는다.

모든, 어떠한	Sit **wherever** you like. = Sit <u>at any place where</u> you like. **Whenever** he goes out, he takes a book. = <u>At any time when</u> he goes out, he takes a book.
양보	**However** you may try, you cannot solve it. = <u>No matter how</u> you may try, you cannot solve it. **Wherever** you are, I will find you. = <u>No matter where</u> you are, I will find you.

Exercise

 ## Exercise 1

둘 중 맞는 단어를 골라 문장을 완성하세요.

❶ Can you let me know　where / when　she will come?

❷ Summer is Harry's favorite season　which / in which　he can swim in the sea.

❸ Nicky and Jane went to the cafe　where / when　they first met each other.

❹ He knows the reason　how / why　she left him.

❺　However / Wherever　he may make a judgment, he will be right.

 ## Exercise 2

주어진 단어들을 바르게 배열해 문장을 완성하세요.

❶ 이 동굴은 구석기인들이 살았던 곳이다.

→ _____.

(lived, is, this, the cave, Paleolithic humans, where)

❷ 그들이 그 일을 마칠 날짜를 정확하게 맞추는 것은 불가능하다.

→ _____.

(the exact date, it, impossible, is, the work, to predict, they, will finish)

❸ 지금이 네가 무엇이든지 시도할 수 있는 때이다.

→ _____.

(anything, now, the time, is, you, when, can try)

✏️ Exercise 3

적절한 관계부사를 사용하여 빈칸을 채워 문장을 완성하세요.

① The wallet is on the table _____ Victoria had her dinner.

② The day on _____ he was born is unknown.

③ I'm curious if you know _____ Jacob didn't come to school today.

④ People often lose their hometown _____ which they built their dreams.

⑤ It is important to remember the reason _____ you work so hard.

⑥ Leaving the place _____ you live is not easy.

Sentence Completion

1. Knowing the way   he can get higher scores, she taught him for 3 years.

   (A) X
   (B) how
   (C) which
   (D) in which

2. To be honest, I really don't care about the reason   they decided to exclude me.

   (A) how
   (B) why
   (C) when
   (D) where

3. Are you sure that you saw them   they were walking across the street?

   (A) how
   (B) why
   (C) when
   (D) which

4. If you give me a chance, I will try my best to find the way   I could make you happy.

   (A) that
   (B) why
   (C) how
   (D) when

5. Tomorrow is the day   we should go on a long adventure to save the world.

   (A) which
   (B) of which
   (C) in which
   (D) for which

6. This is the room   he drew several paintings that we saw yesterday.

   (A) X
   (B) how
   (C) which
   (D) for which

7 Rather than being frustrated by the failure, think about _____ you failed.

(A) when
(B) where
(C) the place
(D) the reason

8 Mr. Brown recommended me to search for the place _____ I can concentrate.

(A) X
(B) why
(C) how
(D) when

9 Little monkey was waiting for _____ he would get his bananas.

(A) X
(B) why
(C) when
(D) the reason

10 Did you find _____ where you can see some shooting stars?

(A) X
(B) why
(C) how
(D) when

11 The professor taught us _____ how we can examine these bacteria.

(A) X
(B) the way
(C) the time
(D) the place

12 I wish I could travel _____ I want with my husband, but I can't.

(A) where
(B) however
(C) wherever
(D) no matter how

Error Recognition

● TOSEL 기출문제 변형 수능/내신 출제유형

틀린 문장 고르기

다음 중 문법적으로 <u>틀린</u> 것을 고르세요.

Soju is a very important part of the drinking culture in Korea. It's affordable. It's everywhere. It goes along with any Korean dishes. Even though Koreans ① **have drunk** Soju since the 14th century, it was not actually invented in Korea. During a time ② **where** the Mongolians had invaded many countries in Asia, they discovered an alcoholic beverage called Arak. ③ **When** Mongolians invaded Korea, they brought Arak with them and introduced this to alcohol makers in Korea. At first, Arak was mostly manufactured in Kaesong and was known as Arak-ju before the name changed to Soju. It was during the time of King Chungryeol ④ **when** drinking Soju became popular among the public. Soju has been consumed ⑤ **for** many years in Korea and has now become a part of Korean identity.

고쳐쓰기

틀린 문장의 번호를 쓰고 올바르게 고치세요.

● TOSEL 기출문제 변형 수능/내신 출제유형

 틀린 문장 고르기

다음 중 문법적으로 <u>틀린</u> 것을 고르세요.

Millions of animals ❶ **are used** for commercial and scientific testing purposes each year. Many types of animals have been used to research the effects of various products and medical techniques. Supporters of animal testing say ❷ **that** it has been a necessary part of advances in medical technology. Without the test on animals, many people would die due to poor medicinal science. ❸ **However**, people against animal testing say that it is unfair to animals because it is inhumane. They argue that the animals experience ❹ **extreme** pain and are treated poorly during testing, ❺ **how** small that animal is. They believe that an alternative method of researching should be used.

 고쳐쓰기

틀린 문장의 번호를 쓰고 올바르게 고치세요.

✏️ 배운 내용 스스로 정리해보기

① 종류와 용법

관계부사의 종류에는 ❶ when, ❷ [   ], ❸ why, ❹ how, ❺ [   ] 이(가) 있고,

이러한 관계부사들은 종류에 따라 ❻ [   ], ❼ [   ] 용법으로 쓰인다.

예시문장 써보기

When의 제한적 용법 → _____

② 관계부사의 생략

예시문장 써보기

관계부사 why가 생략된 문장 → _____

③ 선행사의 생략

예시문장 써보기

'the place'가 생략된 문장 → _____

④ 복합관계부사

❶ [   ] 형태이며, ❷ [   ] 는 복합관계부사로 쓰지 않는다.

예시문장 써보기

whenever의 '모든, 어떠한'의 뜻

→ _____

TOSEL 실전문제 ❺

PART 6. Sentence Completion

DIRECTIONS: In this portion of the test, you will be given 12 incomplete sentences. From the choices provided, choose the word or words that correctly complete the sentence. Then, fill in the corresponding space on your answer sheet.

1. I know a boy _____ father is a famous rockstar.

   (A) who
   (B) whose
   (C) whom
   (D) which

2. Kevin wants to buy a house _____ is located near the forest.

   (A) who
   (B) what
   (C) which
   (D) whose

3. Henry saved the very cat _____ was about to starve to death yesterday.

   (A) that
   (B) what
   (C) who
   (D) of which

4. Nancy was depressed because she couldn't understand _____ her teacher said.

   (A) that
   (B) what
   (C) which
   (D) on which

5. Paul was looking for the woman _____ this purple scarf belongs.

   (A) who
   (B) whom
   (C) where
   (D) to whom

6. The government has planned to build a dam in this town, _____ will drown the town.

   (A) who
   (B) that
   (C) what
   (D) which

7. _____ comes first will be served first.

(A) Who
(B) Whom
(C) Whoever
(D) Whichever

10. He never tells me the day _____ he is going to move back to Hongkong.

(A) how
(B) why
(C) when
(D) where

8. No matter _____ you love, I don't mind as long as you are happy.

(A) how
(B) whom
(C) which
(D) whoever

11. No matter what they say, I love the way _____ he smiles.

(A) X
(B) why
(C) how
(D) which

9. The man _____ you met yesterday is the mayor of New York City.

(A) X
(B) what
(C) which
(D) whose

12. We were best friends back then. I still don't know the reason _____ he got mad at me.

(A) why
(B) how
(C) when
(D) where

Error Recognition

 (1~2) 다음 중 문법적으로 틀린 것을 골라 고치세요.

1

Is a tomato a fruit or a vegetable? According to science, it is a fruit. Yet it **❶ is considered** a vegetable in most countries. There are only a few countries **❷ which** people use tomatoes as fruit. In South Korea, for example, tomatoes **❸ are used** to decorate cakes. They are also often turned into juice, just like grapes or oranges. Someone might **❹ argue** , "Americans drink tomato juice." However, there is an important difference. Americans drink tomato juice **❺ that** is salty or spicy. They consider it as a vegetable juice, not a fruit juice.

 ➜ _____

2

Fork comes from the Latin word furca, meaning "pitchfork." (A pitchfork is a tool ❶ who has two or three thin bars at the end of a long handle.) Forks are ❷ **surprisingly** new compared to spoons and knives. Spoons and knives are ancient eating tools, but people only began ❸ **using** forks a few centuries ago. When forks ❹ **were first introduced** , they were not popular. Many people refused ❺ **to use** them at all. But by the 17th century, more and more people had accepted the fork as an eating tool. Now forks are an everyday part of the dining table.

 ➡ _____

Error Recognition

3

Scones were originally a quick bread **①** (what is) from Scotland. They were made with oats and cooked on a frying pan. Nowadays, scones are often made with flour and baked. Scones became popular in England **②** (because of) the Duchess of Bedford (1788–1861). Late one afternoon, the duchess ordered her servants **③** (to bring) something to snack on. They presented her with a tray of tea and scones. She was so delighted by this **④** (that) she ordered it every afternoon afterwards, at precisely 4 o'clock. Scones continue **⑤** (to be) an important part of the English afternoon tea tradition.

4

Spain's national lottery is also known **①** (as) El Gordo, meaning "the fat one." It is one of **②** (the very oldest) lotteries in the world. Because an entire ticket is expensive, people buy sub-tickets instead. In this way, family members or colleagues can **③** (share) the same ticket. Then on December 22nd, everyone watches the winning number drawn. In 2012, this popular event had an unusual outcome. The entire village of Sodeto won the lottery jackpot! All but one household held at least one piece of a ticket **④** (whom) won the lottery. This meant **⑤** (that) each family received at least €100,000 in prize money.

5

Computer keyboards are based on a layout ❶ `called` QWERTY. This layout was originally designed for typewriters in the early 19th century. It continued ❷ `to be used` even after typewriters were replaced by PCs and their keyboards. But these keyboards were not specifically designed for PCs. They were acceptable for typing words and numbers, but no special keys were ❸ `available` . So in the early 1980s, IBM assembled a group of experts ❹ `to build` a better keyboard. Consequently, the Model M keyboard was invented. The computer keyboards we ❺ `use it` today are still based on this model.

6

It is generally accepted ❶ `that` ice cream cones became popular at the 1904 St. Louis World's Fair. A Syrian immigrant ❷ `what` is named Ernest Hamwi was selling a waffle-like pastry called zalabia at the fair. ❸ `Next to him` was a teenaged ice cream seller named Arnold Fornachou. One busy afternoon, Fornachou ran out of dishes ❹ `to serve` ice cream. Hamwi noticed, and he rolled up some of his zalabia into cones for Fornachou. These edible ice cream cones were a huge hit. Soon other ice cream vendors ❺ `were selling` their ice cream in waffle cones, too.

CHAPTER 6

VI. 가정법

UNIT 01 가정법 현재와 과거   **117**

UNIT 02 가정법 과거완료   **127**

UNIT 03 혼합가정법   **137**

UNIT 04 특수가정법   **147**

TOSEL 실전문제 6   **157**

UNIT 01

가정법 현재와 과거

생김새	**①** **가정법 현재**: 'If + 주어 + 동사의 현재형..., 　　　　　　　　주어 + 조동사의 현재형 + 동사원형...' ex) If I **have** time then, I **will send** you a message. **②** **가정법 과거**: 'If+주어+동사의 과거형…, 　　　　　　　주어+조동사의 과거형+동사원형…' ex) If I **were** a bird, I **could fly** to you.
의미	**①** **가정법 현재**: ~라면, ...할(일) 것이다. **②** **가정법 과거**: ~라면, ...할(일) 텐데. (현재 사실의 반대)

UNIT 1 가정법 현재와 과거

1 가정법 현재와 용법

현재 또는 미래에 대한 가정·상상·소망을 나타내며 동사원형을 사용한다.

명사	The <u>order</u> was that we (should) **wear** uniforms. (= suggestion, requirement, instruction, etc.) 동사원형 The ship carpenter's <u>decision</u> was that we **go** back. (= recommendation, order, etc.) 동사원형
형용사	It is <u>imperative</u> that you (should) **rest** for a month. (= necessary, vital, advisable, important, etc.) 동사원형 It is <u>better</u> that Jack (should) **study** for the test. (= necessary, vital, advisable, etc.) 동사원형
동사	He <u>urged</u> that we (should) **accept** the offer. (= insist, etc.) It is <u>stipulated</u> that the payment (should) **be** in cash. (= require, request, propose, suggest, move, etc.) 동사원형

→ **기원문으로 쓰이는 가정법 현재**

- God **bless** you!
  동사원형
= May God **bless** you!

- Success **attend** you!
  동사원형
= May success **attend** you!

→ **기타 가정법 현재: 'lest'가 이끄는 절**

- He worked hard <u>lest</u> he (should) **fail**.
  동사원형

NOTE 🖉

TIP 직설법 조건문

- If 절에 동사원형을 쓰지 않고 현재형을 쓴다.
- 뜻: 현재 또는 미래에 대한 단순한 조건으로 해석된다.
- If he <u>is</u> honest, I <u>will forgive</u> him.
  현재형   미래형(혹은 현재형)

TIP <u>lest + S + (should) + V</u>

- 뜻: s가 v하지 않기 위해서

② 가정법 과거와 변형

현재 사실의 반대를 가정하거나 실현 불가능한 미래에 대한 소망을 나타낸다.

> If I **were** rich, I **could buy** an airplane.
> 　　　 과거형　　　　 조동사 과거형 + 동사원형
>
> If you **took** the doctor's advice, you **might be** well again soon.
> 　　　 과거형　　　　　　　　　　　　　 조동사 과거형 + 동사원형

could	If you **could** help me, I **would be** very glad. If절의 could: 반드시 현재 사실의 반대인 것은 아님
would	If you **would** send me an e-mail, I **would be** happy. If절의 would: 남이 어떤 일을 해주기를 요구할 때 사용함
형용사절	**Anybody who passed** the park **would see**. = If anybody **passed** the park, he **would see**.

③ 가정법 과거의 관용표현

> ❶ had better, had best + 동사원형
>
> You **had better** go at once.
> 　　　　　　　 현재 가지고 있지 않다는 것을 전제함
>
> ❷ would[had] rather + 동사원형, would[had] sooner
>
> I **would rather** challenge **than** give up.
>
> ❸ as it were
>
> He is, **as it were**, a grown-up baby.
> 　　　 현재 사실의 반대로, 그는 아기가 아니라는 것을 전제함

NOTE

TIP had better + 동사원형
- 뜻: ~하는 편이 좋다. (의무, 충고)

TIP would rather + 동사원형
- 뜻: (차라리) ~ 하겠다. (선호)

TIP as it were
- 뜻: 말하자면, 이를 테면

UNIT 1 가정법 현재와 과거

Exercise

 ## Exercise 1

둘 중 맞는 단어를 골라 문장을 완성하세요.

① If Austin is brave, he will   save / saved   himself.

② The requirement was they   will prepare / prepare   the dinner.

③ It is necessary that you   wash / washed   your hand.

④ If Henry   was / were   handsome, he would be popular.

⑤ You   have / had   better come to my office.

 ## Exercise 2

주어진 단어들을 바르게 배열해 문장을 완성하세요.

① 저 고양이가 울면, 나는 그에게 먹이를 줄 것이다.

➜ _____ .

   (it, if, that cat, I, will, feed, cries)

② Sarah가 이긴다면, 그녀의 기분이 좀 나아질 텐데.

➜ _____ .

   (feel better, she, won, if, Sarah, would, won)

③ 내가 너라면, 나는 포기하지 않을 텐데.

➜ _____ .

   (would, give up, not, if, I, you, I, were, not)

 Exercise 3

주어진 표현을 사용하여 빈칸을 채워 문장을 완성하세요.

1 If my son _____ , I will buy him a car. (graduate)

2 If you _____ a doctor, she would work with you. (be)

3 If she _____ it is unfair, she will complain about it. (think)

4 If they were kind, they _____ a prize from the teacher.
(will receive)

5 I would rather _____ than walk. (run)

6 That man had better _____ first. (apologize)

Sentence Completion

❶ We'll go back inside if the weather _____ below zero.

(A) drop

(B) drops

(C) dropped

(D) dropping

❷ If you _____ now, you'll be too hungry later during class.

(A) ate

(B) don't eat

(C) hadn't eaten

(D) would have

❸ If her friends don't invite her, she _____ on a date with her boyfriend.

(A) go

(B) went

(C) go will

(D) will go

❹ He insisted that we _____ the woman who lived in this town for a long time.

(A) followed

(B) following

(C) follow should

(D) should follow

❺ If Alice listened to her husband, she _____ her disease.

(A) prevented

(B) preventing

(C) could prevent

(D) could prevented

❻ If you _____ kind, you could help that little girl carrying a big bag.

(A) be

(B) are

(C) were

(D) were been

7 If you   sing a song for me, I would be happy enough.

(A) will

(B) were

(C) could

(D) should

8   enjoyed watching movies would know his name.

(A) Which

(B) Whomever

(C) Nobody who

(D) Anybody who

9 They   not ignore what their teacher required them to do.

(A) had best

(B) as it were

(C) would rather

(D) would sooner

10 I   bake some cookies for him than bake some bread.

(A) am best

(B) better had

(C) as it were

(D) would rather

11 Jonny knows everything. He is,   , a walking encyclopedia.

(A) as it were

(B) had better

(C) would rather

(D) would sooner

12 He had better   for his future. He plays computer games for more than 10 hours.

(A) study

(B) studies

(C) studied

(D) should study

UNIT 1 가정법 현재와 과거

Error Recognition

 틀린 문장 고르기

다음 중 문법적으로 <u>틀린</u> 것을 고르세요.

When people are outside for too long in freezing weather, they can get frostbite. In general, frostbite is like a skin burn. However, instead of fire, the cause is cold. The tissues of the skin become covered in ice. This means that blood and oxygen cannot flow ❶ properly . The most common areas for frostbite are the nose, fingers, cheeks, ears, and toes. If a person ❷ gets frostbite, careful treatment is important. A key mistake is rewarming the body part when the victim is still outside in the cold. Rewarming and then refreezing can cause serious damage. It is also important ❸ to know that it hurts to be rewarmed. In fact, among patients with frostbite, there are many cases of damage ❹ caused by such mistakes. If these precautions ❺ are widely known, the number of frostbite patients would be much lower.

 고쳐쓰기

틀린 문장의 번호를 쓰고 올바르게 고치세요.

_____ ➡ _____

 틀린 문장 고르기

다음 중 문법적으로 <u>틀린</u> 것을 고르세요.

Pauline woke up early in the morning because it was a field day at her school. She was so excited. She was supposed to participate in many different games, ❶ **including** badminton, jump rope, baseball, and volleyball. She was most ❷ **excited** about playing volleyball, her favorite sport. On her way to school, however, she fell off her bike and ❸ **hurt** her elbow. It hurt a lot, but she played badminton anyway. As she ❹ **was playing**, her elbow started to bleed. After the badminton game, Sam, her best friend, told her that she had better not ❺ **to play** other games. Sam brought a bandage from a school nurse and put it on Pauline's elbow.

 고쳐쓰기

틀린 문장의 번호를 쓰고 올바르게 고치세요.

✎ 배운 내용 스스로 정리해보기

❶ 가정법 현재와 용법

❶ [   ] 또는 ❷ [   ] 에 대한 가정·상상·소망을 나타낸다.

예시문장 써보기

❶ 직설법 조건문 문장 ➜ _____

❷ suggest를 사용한 문장 ➜ _____

❸ lest가 이끄는 절이 있는 문장 ➜ _____

❷ 가정법 과거와 변형

❶ [   ] 을(를) 가정하거나 ❷ [   ] 에 대한 소망을 나타낸다.

예시문장 써보기

❶ If절에 be동사의 과거형 사용 ➜ _____

❷ If절에 would 사용 ➜ _____

❸ 가정법 과거의 관용표현

예시문장 써보기

❶ had better + 동사원형 ➜ _____

❷ as it were ➜ _____

UNIT 02

가정법 과거완료

생김새	'**If + 주어 + had + p.p** **주어 + 조동사의 과거형 + have + p.p'** ex) If you **had drunk** iced coffee, 　　you **would have studied** till late at night.
의미	~했더라면(이었다면), ...했었을(이었을) 텐데.
쓰임	과거의 사실을 반대로 가정할 때 ex) If she **had taken** shower fast, 　　she **would not have been** late for school. ex) If he **had known** the answer, 　　he **would not have struggled** with the problem.

❶ 가정법 과거완료의 기본

과거 사실과 반대되는 가정을 나타낸다.

If the weather **hadn't been** so bad, we **would have gone** out.
　　　　　　　　　과거완료형　　　　　　　　　　　조동사 과거형 + 현재완료형

If Lucy **had come**, I **would have been** grateful.
　　　　　　과거완료형　　　조동사 과거형 + 현재완료형

If there **hadn't been** Sam, she **wouldn't have participated**.
　　　　　　　과거완료형　　　　　　　　　　조동사 과거형 + 현재완료형

If you **hadn't been** there, you **wouldn't have known** how traumatic it was.
　　　　과거완료형　　　　　　　　조동사 과거형 + 현재완료형

➜ **(비교)직설법 조건문 대과거: 과거사실의 반대가 아니다.**

• If I **had been alarmed** before, I **was embarrassed** yesterday.
　　　과거완료형　　　　　　　　　　　과거형

• If he **had been disappointed** before, he **was enraged** this morning.
　　　　과거완료형　　　　　　　　　　　　　과거형

---

② 가정법 과거완료의 변형

could have p.p	If he <u>could have helped</u>, I **should have done** it.
	If I <u>could have called</u> her, I **should have met** her.
	If she <u>could have made</u> it on time, I **should have got** on the train.
	If my brother <u>could have stayed</u>, I **should have gone** to the zoo.

➡ 단, **would have p.p**는 못 쓴다.

- If you **would have given** that, I **would have been** glad. (X)

➡ If you **had given** that, I **would have been** glad. (O)
　　　　과거완료형　　　　　조동사 과거형 + 현재완료형

- If you **would have called** him, I **would have been** angry. (X)

➡ If you **had called** him, I **would have been** angry. (O)
　　　　과거완료형　　　　　조동사 과거형 + 현재완료형

UNIT 2 가정법 과거완료

Exercise

 ## Exercise 1

둘 중 맞는 단어를 골라 문장을 완성하세요.

---

1 If she had studied, she would   **has received / have received**   better score.

2 If this place had   **be / been**   bigger, they would have come.

3 If they   **could / would**   have called him, they should have met him.

4 If he   **has / had**   launched the missile, people would have died.

5 If Olive had married Maison, they would have   **live / lived**   in Seoul.

 ## Exercise 2

주어진 단어들을 바르게 배열해 문장을 완성하세요.

---

1 네가 왔다면, 너는 놀랐을 텐데.

→ _____ .

(have been, had come, you, you, would, surprised, if)

2 내가 선생님이 됐었다면, 나는 과학을 가르쳤을 텐데.

→ _____ .

(if, had become, I, I, would have, science, taught, a teacher)

3 Grace가 이사를 했었다면, 그녀는 새로운 직장을 찾았을 텐데.

→ _____ .

(moved, she would, if Grace, had, found, a new job, have)

 Exercise 3

주어진 단어를 활용하여 빈칸을 채워 문장을 완성하세요.

❶ If you hadn't been there, I wouldn't have _____ you. (know)

❷ If Baker had _____ the book, he would have been famous. (write)

❸ If students hadn't agreed, they wouldn't have _____ the exam. (take)

❹ If I had eaten the cake, she would have _____ angry at me. (be)

❺ If I could have called my mom, I should have _____ her halfway. (meet)

❻ If she could have _____ faster, she should have escaped from there. (run)

Sentence Completion

1 If _____ it would be raining, we never would have started this hike.

(A) had we known

(B) we had known

(C) known we had

(D) had known we

2 If you _____, you would have not only achieved your goal but also won the prize.

(A) given hadn't up

(B) hadn't given up

(C) hadn't up given

(D) given up hadn't

3 If I had taken a picture with him, I _____ it to my parents.

(A) will had shown

(B) will have shown

(C) would had shown

(D) would have shown

4 If that soldier had seen the plane, they _____ it down.

(A) would have shot

(B) shot would have

(C) would have shoot

(D) would shoot have

5 If they had shouted, their teacher _____ them to be quiet.

(A) would have told

(B) would told have

(C) have told would

(D) told would have

6 If Jane had accepted his request, she _____ a lot of money.

(A) would had earn

(B) would have earn

(C) would had earned

(D) would have earned

7 If you _____ to be a singer, you would have practiced more.

(A) are dream

(B) are dreaming

(C) had dreamed

(D) have dreamed

10 If I _____ this group project a little earlier, I should have met her at the airport.

(A) could have finished

(B) should have finished

(C) should finished had

(D) could finished had

8 _____ my teeth well, I wouldn't have needed to go to the dentist.

(A) I had brushed

(B) I have brushed

(C) If I had brushed

(D) If I have brushed

11 If we _____ less, we should have finished our homework.

(A) could have slept

(B) could slept have

(C) should have slept

(D) should slept have

9 If someone had given me a ride, I _____ to the concert.

(A) will go

(B) will gone

(C) would have going

(D) would have gone

12 If you could have been more patient, you _____ more marshmallows.

(A) must received have

(B) must have received

(C) should received have

(D) should have received

UNIT 2 가정법 과거완료

Error Recognition

 틀린 문장 고르기

다음 중 문법적으로 <u>틀린</u> 것을 고르세요.

Penguins, like ostriches, have wings but cannot fly. In the old days, however, their ancestors ❶ could fly. Over millions of years, penguins have evolved. As they evolved, they lost their ability ❷ to fly . A flying bird usually has hollow bones to make it lighter. But over time, penguins' bones became ❸ solid and heavy. Now, they cannot lift themselves out of the water to fly. However, with their heavier bones, they can now dive down into the water. Penguins can dive to depths of 1000m and ❹ remain underwater for up to 20 minutes. If they ❺ haven't evolved, the penguins would have moved by flying instead of swimming.

 고쳐쓰기

틀린 문장의 번호를 쓰고 올바르게 고치세요.

⟶ _____

 틀린 문장 고르기

다음 중 문법적으로 <u>틀린</u> 것을 고르세요.

The Bayeux Tapestry is a long cloth with images sewn into it. It shows historical events ❶ **related** to a group from Normandy, France, who had a battle with England. It was probably made in the 11th century, a few years after an important battle. The total tapestry has fifty scenes on it. The most important battle and action scenes are in the center of the tapestry. The Bayeux Tapestry ❷ **has modified** many times over history. For example, an extra cloth was added to the back of it in 1724. Around the year 1800, numbers were put on the cloth to help ❸ **array** the scenes. The front of the tapestry has also been fixed a little. But sadly, the end of the tapestry is likely missing. Researchers think that the tapestry originally ❹ **had** 1.5 extra meters. If the end of the tapestry had been intact, we could ❺ **have known** more history.

 고쳐쓰기

틀린 문장의 번호를 쓰고 올바르게 고치세요.

배운 내용 스스로 정리해보기

① 가정법 과거완료의 기본

       와(과) 반대되는 가정을 나타낸다.

예시문장 써보기

❶ 날씨가 좋지 않았더라면, ~

➜ _____

❷ 내가 공부를 열심히 하지 않았더라면, ~

➜ _____

❸ 그가 바쁘지 않았더라면, ~

➜ _____

② 가정법 과거완료의 변형

예시문장 써보기

If절에 could have p.p. 사용

➜ _____

UNIT 03

혼합가정법

생김새	❶ **가정법 과거 + 가정법 과거완료**
	ex) If my memory were bad,
	I <u>**would not have remembered**</u> the situation.
	❷ **가정법 과거완료 + 가정법 과거**
	ex) If he <u>**had missed**</u> the train,
	he <u>**would not be**</u> here now.
	❸ **가정법과 직설법의 혼합**
	ex) <u>**It is time**</u> you <u>**went**</u> to school.
의미	**주절과 종속절[If절]의 시제가 다르다.**

UNIT 3 혼합가정법

❶ 가정법 혼합시제

If절과 주절의 시제가 내용상 서로 다른 경우, 혼합시제를 쓴다.

> **❶ If절** (가정법 과거완료형 동사) **+ 주절** (가정법 과거형 조동사)

If it **had not rained** yesterday, it **wouldn't be** cold today.
　　　　　과거완료형　　　　　　　　　　　　　조동사 과거형 + 현재형

= As it **rained** yesterday, it **is** so cold today.

> **❷ If절** (가정법 과거형 동사) **+ 주절** (가정법 과거완료형 조동사)

If he **did not make** mistakes, how **could** it **have been** broken?
　　　　過거형　　　　　　　　　　　　조동사 과거형 + 과거완료형

= As he **makes** mistakes, it **could be** broken.

❷ 직설법과 가정법이 혼합된 문장

❶ It is time (직설법 문장) + 가정법 문장

It is time you **went** to bed.
　　　　　　　　　과거형
= **It is time** you should go to bed.
　　　　　　　should: ~해야 하는데 하고 있지 않다는 뜻의 당연·재촉을 의미함
= **It is time** for you to go to bed.

It is time he **was[were]** up.
　　　　　　was: 대명사 뒤에서 우선함

❷ I wish (직설법 문장) + 가정법 문장

I **wish** it **were** true. 현재사실에 반대되는 소원

I **wish** it **had been** true. 과거사실에 반대되는 소원

I **wished** it **were** true. 과거사실에 반대되는 과거소원

I **wished** it **had been** true. 대과거사실에 반대되는 과거소원

I **wish** you **would** not keep interrupting me. 미래에 실현하기 어려운 소망
= I **would rather** you not keep interrupting me.

→ **If only**

- **If only the rain would stop.** 미래의 실현하기 어려운 소망
= I wish the rain would stop.

- **If only he comes in time.** 단순한 미래의 소망
= I hope he will come in time.

❸ 직설법 문장 + as if[as though] + 가정법 문장

가정법 문장	He **talks** <u>as if</u> he **knew** everything. He **talks** <u>as if</u> he **had known** everything. He **talked** <u>as if</u> he **knew** everything. He **talked** <u>as if</u> he **had known** everything.
직설법 문장	He looks <u>as if</u> he **is** sick. 사실적 표현 = He seems to be sick.
생략	You can behave <u>as if</u> **(you were)** a kid.

Exercise

Exercise 1

둘 중 맞는 단어를 골라 문장을 완성하세요.

1 If she had exercised last month, she would be / had been thin now.

2 If Erick hadn't seen her last year, he wouldn't marry / had married her today.

3 It is time you wake / woke up.

4 If only the weather will / would be fine.

5 He acts as if / if as he were a doctor.

Exercise 2

주어진 단어들을 바르게 배열해 문장을 완성하세요.

1 어제 구름이 끼지 않았다면, 오늘 바람이 불지 않을 텐데.

→ _____.

(had, been, it, not, if, be windy today, cloudy yesterday, wouldn't, it)

2 우리가 집에 가야 할 시간이다.

→ _____.

(time, we, it, home, is, went)

3 나는 내가 과학자이기를 바란다.

→ _____.

(wish, I, I, a scientist, were)

주어진 단어를 활용하여 빈칸을 채워 문장을 완성하세요.

1 If it had been warm last night, they wouldn't _____ sick today. (be)

2 It is time you should _____ your homework. (finish)

3 I wish he would not _____ me. (forget)

4 I wished you had _____ my efforts. (know)

5 If only she _____ our anniversary. (remember)

6 They seem as if they _____ hungry. (be)

Sentence Completion

① If I _____ slept better last night, I wouldn't be so tired now.

(A) am

(B) had

(C) have

(D) should have

② If you had asked for her phone number last week, you would _____ able to call her today.

(A) be

(B) are

(C) had

(D) have

③ If I _____ been friends with her for a long time, I would help her this afternoon.

(A) had

(B) having

(C) should had

(D) should have

④ If I had made a reservation _____, she wouldn't be angry today.

(A) now

(B) today

(C) yesterday

(D) tomorrow

⑤ If it had rained last night, the road would be slippery _____.

(A) yesterday

(B) last week

(C) this morning

(D) the day before yesterday

⑥ It is time the drivers _____, but they couldn't because of the bad weather.

(A) arrive

(B) arrived

(C) had arrive

(D) have arrive

7 I wish _____ smart enough to solve the problem.

(A) they had
(B) had they
(C) they were
(D) were they

10 I'm sorry. I wish I _____ chocolate, but I don't.

(A) like
(B) liked
(C) will like
(D) had liked

8 Melly wishes her younger brother would _____ to her well.

(A) listen
(B) listened
(C) had listened
(D) have listened

11 The children talk as if they had _____ what their parents told them.

(A) forget
(B) forgot
(C) forgotten
(D) forgottening

9 _____ you understand your parent's mind.

(A) If
(B) only
(C) Only if
(D) If only

12 Two girls taking a bus look as if they _____ a cold.

(A) had
(B) have
(C) having
(D) had have

Error Recognition

 틀린 문장 고르기

다음 중 문법적으로 <u>틀린</u> 것을 고르세요.

Placed on the first list of UNESCO World Heritage Sites, the Wieliczka Salt Mine in Poland opened in the 13th century. Since the mid-1990s it has no longer been a working mine ① **due to** globally lowered salt prices. Instead, the Wieliczka Salt Mine is like an art-filled historical site lit by romantic lamps. It has a full cathedral in it, with statues and prayer places made out of salt that ② **was carved** by the miners who worked there. One of the most fascinating things about the mine ③ **are** that it contains a giant lamp made of rock salt. It looks ④ **as if** it is one huge artwork. It is very deep and ⑤ **extremely** long: not 100 kilometers, or even 200 kilometers, but an astounding 287 kilometers!

 고쳐쓰기

틀린 문장의 번호를 쓰고 올바르게 고치세요.

[   ] ➡ _____

 틀린 문장 고르기

다음 중 문법적으로 <u>틀린</u> 것을 고르세요.

The history of running shoes is not very long. In the past, athletes wore leather shoes. The leather shoes stretched if they got wet. Also, the shoes were hard, so they hurt people's feet. In 1832, however, Wait Webster found a way ❶ **to attach** rubber onto the bottom of leather shoes. The shoes were mainly just for children. But these were the first running shoes with rubber soles. Twenty years later, a British company attached sharp spikes onto their shoes. The spikes made it ❷ **easier** to run, especially on grass. By the 1890s, many factories ❸ **were making** rubber. Soon sports companies started to connect rubber soles together with canvas material. This process made a very light shoe. Runners could easily run in such shoes. Since the 19th century, technology ❹ **has changed** running shoes. If past athletes and sports companies had not ❺ **went** through trial and error, there wouldn't be comfortable running shoes today.

 고쳐쓰기

틀린 문장의 번호를 쓰고 올바르게 고치세요.

  ➡ _____

UNIT 3 혼합가정법

배운 내용 스스로 정리해보기

① 가정법 혼합시제

If절과 주절의 시제가 내용상 서로   경우, 혼합시제를 쓴다.

예시문장 써보기

❶ 가정법 과거 + 가정법 과거완료

➜ _____

❷ 가정법 과거완료 + 가정법 과거

➜ _____

② 직설법과 가정법이 혼합된 문장

예시문장 써보기

❶ It is time + 가정법 과거 문장

➜ _____

❷ I wish + 가정법 과거 문장 (현재사실에 반대되는 소원)

➜ _____

❸ I wish + 가정법 과거완료 문장(과거사실에 반대되는 소원)

➜ _____

❹ 직설법 문장 + as if[as though] + 가정법 문장

➜ _____

UNIT 04

특수가정법

> **쓰임**
>
> ❶ **if의 생략**: 'were · had · should · had + p.p'가 있는 if 조건절에서 if를 생략하면 'were · had · should'가 도치됨
>
> ex) **Were** I a bird, I would fly to you.
>
> ❷ **if의 대용**: 분사, 접속사, 부정사, 부사어구, 전치사(구), 주어 · 형용사절, 조건절 또는 주절이 if를 대신함
>
> ex) **Providing[Provided]** that you <u>are</u> my colleague, you may not be jealous of me.

UNIT **4** 특수가정법

① If의 생략

Were I rich, I would buy a car.
　동사 주어

= If I were rich, I would buy a car.

Should it rain tomorrow, I would postpone it.
　동사　　主어

= If it should rain tomorrow, I would postpone it.

Had you asked me, I would have told you the answer.
　동사 주어

= If you had asked me, I would have told you the answer.

➡ **일반동사의 가정법 과거 경우에는 If를 생략할 수 없다.**

· If I knew myself, I would not make such a mistake.

≠ Did I know myself, I would not make such a mistake. (X)

NOTE ✏

② If의 대용

분사	**Left to herself,** she would have gone astray. = If she had been left alone, she would have gone astray.
접속사	**Providing that it is done,** you may go home. = Provided that it is done, you may go home. **Suppose you are late,** what excuse will you make? **Supposing** he knew it, what would he say?
부정사	I should be happy **to accompany you.** = I should be happy if I could accompany you.
부사어구	I ran, **otherwise** I should have missed the plane. = If I hadn't run, I should have missed the plane. He could have done it **with your help.** = He could have done it if he had had your help.
전치사(구)	If it were not **for him,** I would not go there.
주어· 형용사절	**A wise man** would not do such a thing. = If he were a wise man, he would not do such a thing. ≠ A wise man will not do such a thing. **습성/경향의 will** **A man who had common sense** would do it. = A man, if he had common sense, would do it.
조건절· 주절	If he were alive now! ^{조건절} That would seem strange. ^{주절}

NOTE

TIP If절을 대신하는 전치사(구)

- If it were not for
= Were it not for
= If there were no
= Without
= But[Except] for

- If it had not been for
= Had it not been for
= If there had been no
= Without
= But[Except] for

UNIT 4 특수가정법

Exercise

Exercise 1

둘 중 맞는 단어를 골라 문장을 완성하세요.

1. **Am / Were** I you, I would not leave.

2. **Have / Had** you called me, I would have listened to you.

3. **Should / Could** it be cold next week, he would buy a coat.

4. They should be sad **could / to** know the news.

5. **A brave man / If a brave man** would succeed.

Exercise 2

주어진 단어들을 바르게 배열해 문장을 완성하세요.

1. 내 키가 더 크다면, 나는 농구선수가 될 텐데.

   → _____.

   (I, I, were, be, would, taller, a basketball player)

2. 그녀가 아니라면, 너는 늦지 않을 텐데.

   → _____.

   (you, if, not be late, would, for her, it, were not)

3. 우리는 그녀의 가르침으로 그것을 성취할 수 있었다.

   → _____.

   (could, it, have accomplished, we, her teaching, with)

 Exercise 3

주어진 단어를 활용하여 빈칸을 채워 문장을 완성하세요.

① _____ you need more information, you can contact us at 555-7585. (Shall)

② _____ I wise, I would employ her. (Be)

③ _____ she been rich, she would have entered private school. (Have)

④ _____ he praised her, she would have been happier. (Have)

⑤ I endured, otherwise I should have _____ through it again. (go)

⑥ _____ it not for you, I would not be able to graduate. (be)

Sentence Completion

1 ⬤   simply asked someone for directions, we would not be lost now.

(A) We had

(B) Had we

(C) If had we

(D) If we would

4 ⬤   the truth, they would not have given a trophy to him.

(A) They had

(B) They known

(C) Had they known

(D) If they had know

2 ⬤   forgiven Taylor, they would have been good friends.

(A) Had he

(B) He had

(C) If had he

(D) If he should

5 ⬤   it rain tonight, he would come to pick me up.

(A) Will

(B) Could

(C) Would

(D) Should

3 ⬤   he here, he woudl lead the discussion skillfully.

(A) Is

(B) Was

(C) Did

(D) Were

6 ⬤   created a time machine, I would have found my mother.

(A) We had

(B) If we had

(C) If had we

(D) If we should

7 _____ more careful, they would not have made such a mistake.

(A) If they be
(B) If they are
(C) Had they be
(D) Had they been

8 _____ Ella's advice, I would not get deceived by Summer.

(A) Took I
(B) If I take
(C) If I took
(D) Did I take

9 _____ had scientific knowledge would understand it.

(A) If student
(B) A student
(C) If a student
(D) A student who

10 _____ you find the cat on the road starving, what would you do?

(A) Suppose
(B) Supposed
(C) Of suppose
(D) To suppose

11 _____ that it is agreed by everyone in this classroom, you may start the project.

(A) Provide
(B) Provided
(C) To provide
(D) For provide

12 He _____ have won the election with his family's passionate support.

(A) are
(B) could
(C) are to
(D) is able to

Error Recognition

● TOSEL 기출문제 변형 수능/내신 출제유형

 틀린 문장 고르기

다음 중 문법적으로 <u>틀린</u> 것을 고르세요.

Oliver's favorite band **①** **was having** a concert. To buy tickets, Oliver had to line up overnight with his friend, **②** **starting** from the early evening. Late at night, he got bored in the line. He put a sign with his name on it in his spot. Then, he went to his car **③** **to sleep** . Finally, he woke up and returned to the line, but his sign **④** **was gone** . When he tried to go back to his spot, people got really angry. As a result, Oliver had to go back to the end of the line. Hours later, he got to the ticket window. But by the time he got there, all the tickets were gone. Not **⑤** **going** back to his car, he could have bought a ticket.

 고쳐쓰기

틀린 문장의 번호를 쓰고 올바르게 고치세요.

→ _____

 틀린 문장 고르기

다음 중 문법적으로 <u>틀린</u> 것을 고르세요.

Milo's hockey bags are full. He has his own skates and a good hockey stick ① **that** was his older sister's. The bottom of the stick ② **is wrapped** in strong black tape. He also has shoulder pads to protect his chest and shoulders. Milo thinks those stiff pads make him hard ③ **to move** . Despite these inconveniences, he always wears them. When he fell in his first game, his shoulder pads prevented the injury. ④ **Not had he** worn it, he would have been badly hurt. Of course, he also has a strong helmet. Under the helmet, Milo wears a mouth guard to protect his teeth. In short, Milo's hockey bags contain a lot of safety equipment ⑤ **to help** him play hockey.

 고쳐쓰기

틀린 문장의 번호를 쓰고 올바르게 고치세요.

✏️ 배운 내용 스스로 정리해보기

① If의 생략

❶ [   ] 에 'were · had · should · had + p.p.'가 있을 때 if를 생략하면 'were · had · should'가 ❷ [   ] 된다. 단, ❸ [   ] 은(는) ❹ [   ] 될 수 없다.

예시문장 써보기

❶ 'were'의 도치 ➜ _____

❷ 'had'의 도치 ➜ _____

❸ 'should'의 도치 ➜ _____

② If의 대용

예시문장 써보기

❶ 'Providing[Provided]' 사용

➜ _____

❷ 'If it had not been for' 사용

➜ _____

❸ 'Had it not been for' 사용

➜ _____

❹ 'But[Except] for' 사용

➜ _____

❺ 'Without' 사용

➜ _____

TOSEL 실전문제 ❻

PART 6. Sentence Completion

DIRECTIONS: In this portion of the test, you will be given 12 incomplete sentences. From the choices provided, choose the word or words that correctly complete the sentence. Then, fill in the corresponding space on your answer sheet.

1. The protesters strongly insisted that Asians not _____ discriminated.

    (A) be
    (B) are
    (C) were
    (D) should

2. If I _____ 10 years younger, I would travel all around the world.

    (A) be
    (B) am
    (C) were
    (D) were been

3. I _____ have Italian than Chinese food today. I had dimsum yesterday.

    (A) had best
    (B) as it were
    (C) had better
    (D) would rather

4. If Ted had been on time, the party _____ earlier.

    (A) start
    (B) started
    (C) would start
    (D) would have started

5. If Jamie _____ then, she would have moved to New York.

    (A) marry
    (B) married
    (C) had married
    (D) have married

6. Anyone who had not completed the project would _____ penalized.

    (A) be
    (B) was
    (C) have been
    (D) have being

7. If I _____ in university then, I would be a sophomore now.

   (A) enroll
   (B) enrolled
   (C) had enrolled
   (D) had been enrolled

8. It's time something _____ about environmental issues and global warming.

   (A) do
   (B) did
   (C) had done
   (D) was done

9. I wish I _____ so much money buying clothes yesterday. Now I am totally broke.

   (A) hadn't spent
   (B) didn't spend
   (C) haven't spent
   (D) weren't spent

10. _____ go back to Korea, be sure to call me as soon as you arrive.

    (A) You should
    (B) Should you
    (C) You should have
    (D) Should have you

11. _____ you finish your homework before dinner, I will let you stay out late.

    (A) Provide
    (B) Provided
    (C) To provide
    (D) For providing

12. _____ not been for his help, I would've been robbed and beaten by a burglar.

    (A) It were
    (B) Were it
    (C) Had it
    (D) It had

Error Recognition

 (1~2) 다음 중 문법적으로 틀린 것을 골라 고치세요.

1

Drawings on Christmas cards often show us Santa and his reindeer **1** flying across the night sky. In the background, a full moon is shining. This Christmas image is iconic, but it is misleading. A full moon at Christmas, **2** known as the "full cold moon," is a rare event. It only happens every 19 years. It is, **3** as it was , hard to say that this is the icon of Christmas. The most recent Christmas moon occurred in 2015. The next opportunity **4** to see a Christmas moon won't be until 2034. Interestingly, Koreans call this the "lucky moon." They believe **5** that seeing such a rare full moon will bring good luck.

2

For most of its history, Pattaya was a tiny fishing village. But things began to change for Pattaya in the late 1950s. At that time, American troops ❶ **were stationed** in Thailand because of the Vietnam War. One group of soldiers had a week-long break from their duties, and they ended up in Pattaya. After ❷ **returning** to base, these soldiers talked about how great Pattaya had been. More and more American soldiers began to visit, ❸ **so** Pattaya grew quickly. Soon restaurants and hotels moved in, ❹ **replacing** the local fishing huts and shops. If there hadn't been the soldiers, Pattaya wouldn't ❺ **have** a major tourist destination.

 → _____

Error Recognition

 (3~6) 다음 중 문법적으로 틀린 것을 고르세요.

● TOSEL 기출문제 변형 수능/내신 출제유형

3

Plaque, the stuff we want ❶ **to remove** from our teeth, is like peanut butter. It's thick and sticky and won't ❷ **wash** off easily. So what really cleans our teeth? A toothbrush and floss do. Brushing reaches about 70% of tooth surfaces. Around once a week, clean your teeth with a dry toothbrush (no toothpaste, no water). ❸ **Brush** your teeth and along the gum line in gentle circles. Afterward, put a small amount of toothpaste on your toothbrush. Use this to brush your tongue, not your teeth. ❹ **Did you do** this steadily, you would not have to visit the dentist. This is the best cleaning ❺ **that** you can do in between dentist visits!

● TOSEL 기출문제 변형 수능/내신 출제유형

4

Do you ever feel sick and dizzy while riding on a bus or boat? This ❶ **is called** motion sickness. Tim Flaxman, a British farmer, used to suffer from severe motion sickness. For most of his life, he couldn't ❷ **travel** very far because of it. But by chance, he discovered a solution. While on a train, he found that ❸ **covering** one of his eyes stopped his nausea. Soon after, he designed special sunglasses to prevent motion sickness. These sunglasses have one lens ❹ **that** lets the wearer see light, but no movement. Because the motion signals are blocked, the wearer's motion sickness stops. If this accidental discovery ❺ **did not** happened, there would still be many motion sickness patients who are reluctant to travel far.

5

Cancún was once a deserted island. Its name is believed to be from the Mayan language and roughly translates as "a nest of snakes." That name ❶ **had looked** as if it was full of snakes. However, Cancún was not actually full of snakes. Instead, it was filled ❷ **with** fruit trees, exotic flowers and colorful animals. Other than a few pirates, the place remained ❸ **uninhabited** for a long time. Things changed for Cancún in the 1970s. In 1968, the Mexican government made a national development plan. It chose Cancún for development, and the first resort ❹ **there** opened in 1974. Cancún was quickly ❺ **transformed**. It is now a major tourist destination in Mexico.

6

Every November, my company ❶ **has** a thank you dinner for all the employees. During the year, we mostly meet with our own team and don't get to talk ❷ **to** people from other departments. Once a year, though, the ❸ **entire** company gets together for a big meal. It is stipulated by the company policy that all employees ❹ **participated**. It's a nice way ❺ **to make** us all feel like we are part of one big team.

수능 대비 문제

Answers

Short Answers

UNIT 1 p.24

Exercise 1
1. recognized   2. disappointed   3. was eaten   4. found   5. was asked

Exercise 2
1. The paper was torn.   2. The ice cream is covered with chocolate.   3. The cloth Ella is wearing is made by Bill.

Exercise 3
1. was caught   2. is broken   3. is engaged   4. were born   5. were called   6. is considered

Sentence completion p.26
1. (C) injured   2. (C) intrigued   3. (B) was   4. (A) need   5. (A) was hung   6. (C) were created
7. (D) was frozen   8. (B) be held   9. (A) call   10. (D) was known   11. (B) was given   12. (D) was taken

Error Recognition p.28
1. (5) take   2. (5) take → taken
1. (3) testing   2. (3) testing → tested

Unit Review p.30
❶ 동작의 행위자   ❷ 수동태의 주어   ❸ 행위자   ❹ 동일한 주어   ❺ 감정, 피해, 종사, 출생

❶ The building was built in 1980's.   ❷ English is spoken in America (by Americans).   ❸ The eroor was made (by me).   ❹ The window was broken (by Jason).   ❺ He is famous and is regarded as a promising singer.

❻ 감정 ➡ I was worried about the man.   피해 ➡ The town was destroyed.

종사 ➡ She is enagaged in export.   출생 ➡ We were born in New York.

UNIT 2 p.34

Exercise 1
1. resembles   2. Let   3. was witnessed   4. By whom   5. was given

Exercise 2
1. The lion caught the rabbit.   2. Jack gave Susan a brithday present.   3. his parents called him Charlie.

Exercise 3
1. Chocolate flavored marshmallows are loved by me.   2. Books were borrowed by you.   3. The player was praised by the manager.
4. She is called the genius by everyone in our class.   5. A teddy bear is bought for the little child by the rich man.   6. Nick's wife is given a ring by Nick. / A ring is given to Nick's wife by Nick.

Sentence completion p.36
1. (C) given   2. (A) have   3. (D) was recommended   4. (B) costs   0. (A) reveal   6. (C) was known
7. (C) is elected   8. (D) By whom   9. (D) being used   10. (D) Don't let   11. (C) not be moved   12. (C) be cleaned

Error Recognition p.38
1. (2) was revealed   2. (2) was revealed → revealed
1. (4) made   2. (4) made → is made

Unit Review p.40
1. ❶ S + be V + p.p + ~ + by 목적격

❶ The schedule was canceled by them   ❷ I was sent the document by her. / The document was sent (to) me.   ❸ She is called a genius by us.

2. ❶ 의문문   ❷ 명령문

❶ By whom was this phenomenon explained?   ❷ Let all the manuals be memorized.

UNIT 3 p.44

Exercise 1
1. with   2. to   3. at   4. for   5. about

Exercise 2
1. Susan was worried about her test score.   2. Bob was totally immersed in watching birds fly.   3. The missing boy was found by the police.

Exercise 3
1. was satisfied with   2. is known for   3. were surprised at   4. was delighted with   5. was cancled by   6. is worried about

Sentence completion p.46
1. (D) with   2. (C) surprised   3. (D) about   4. (C) for   5. (A) in   6. (A) known
7. (C) at   8. (B) by   9. (D) satisfied with   10. (C) worried about   11. (B) in   12. (B) for

Error Recognition p.48
1. (3) was pleased   2. (3) was pleased → was pleased with
1. (1) is known to   2. (1) is known to → is known as

Unit Review p.50
1. ❶ by   ❷ to   ❸ at   ❹ in   ❺ for   ❻ with

❼ about

❶ The editorial was criticized by her.   ❷ The email will be sent to you immediately.

❸ Jenny was excited at the musical.   ❹ They were involved in the accident.

❺ The park is known for its beautiful landscape.   ❻ She was satisfied with the results.

❼ I was concerned about my health.

UNIT 4 p.54 ► Exercise 1	🖉	1. taken care of by	2. to be	3. to leave	4. anybody	5. hidden	
► Exercise 2	🖉	1. The king was looked up to by his people.		2. Tina was seen to jog in the morning.		3. All electronic devices should be turned off before the movie starts.	
► Exercise 3	🖉	1. was seen to	2. gets accustomed to	3. is said to	4. are taken care of by	5. buried	6. not satisfied
► Sentence completion p.56	🖉	1. (B) that	2. (D) to be	3. (D) care of by	4. (A) laughed at	5. (D) be pulled	6. (B) be submitted
		7. (A) anybody	8. (C) anybody	9. (D) to help	10. (C) to quit	11. (C) became	12. (D) remained
► Error Recognition p.58	🖉	1. (3) was only lasted		2. (3) was only lasted → only lasts			
	🖉	1. (2) pull apart		2. (2) pull apart → be pulled apart			
► Unit Review p.60	🖉	1. ➡ It is beliebed that a life is similar to a journey.		2. ➡ He was caught up with by her.		3. ➡ The print should be fixed by them.	
		4. ➡ The change would not be noticed by anybody.		5. ❶ She was seen to take a taxi.		❷ We were made to wear school uniform.	
		6. ➡ We got married last month.					
TOSEL 실전문제 4	🖉	1. (D) about	2. (C) are used	3. (D) were delayed	4. (C) was disappointed	5. (C) existed	6. (D) being said
		7. (C) for	8. (B) located	9. (C) be protected	10. (A) is said that	11. (D) anybody	12. (C) to do
	🖉	1. (4) has canceled → has been canceled			2. (1) is well known to → is well known for		
		3. (2) is choosing	4. (2) carefully picked	5. (5) born		6. (3) including	

CHAPTER 5 — p.68

UNIT 1 p.72 ► Exercise 1	🖉	1. who	2. which	3. whose	4. whom	5. who	
► Exercise 2	🖉	1. I saved the boy who was about to faint.		2. You can use the computer which he brought.		3. Noa is a little girl whose hair is short.	
► Exercise 3	🖉	1. They are friends who knew each other for 10 years.		2. He has a ring which is bold.		3. She wants to visit her teacher whose eyes are big.	
		4. Olive met a strong man whom she fell in love with.		5. Chris is handsome, which Fredrick is not.		6. He is wearing a hat whose color is blue.	
► Sentence completion p.74	🖉	1. (A) who	2. (C) who	3. (C) whom	4. (D) whose	5. (B) which	6. (B) which
		7. (D) whose	8. (B) which	9. (B) that	10. (A) that	11. (A) that	12. (C) that
► Error Recognition p.76	🖉	1. (4) whose		2. (4) whose → who			
	🖉	1. (4) that		2. (4) that → which			
► Unit Review p.78	🖉	1. ❶ who	❷ whose	❸ whom	❹ which	❺ of which	❻ which
		➡ I miss my friend whom I met last Christmas.					
	🖉	2. ❶ 앞 문장의 일부 또는 전체		➡ It's peak season again, whiich means we'll be working around the clock.			
	🖉	3. ❶ 한정적 [제한적]		➡ This is the restaurant that serves pizza.			
UNIT 2 p.82 ► Exercise 1	🖉	1. what	2. what	3. who	4. what	5. who	
► Exercise 2	🖉	1. Bob was being chased by the man, who had a scary face.		2. You know what should be done first.		3. The movie's topic is the one that I am afraid of.	
► Exercise 3	🖉	1. This is the thing which[that] she asked me to do.		2. Julia is not the one that she dreamed to be.		3. The thing which[that] you said cannot be true.	
		4. People tend to judge others with the thing which[that] one has.		5. Don't let them take the thing which[that] you deserve to get.		6. The thing which[that] Ilay gave his teacher is his essay.	
► Sentence completion p.84	🖉	1. (C) what	2. (B) what	3. (D) what	4. (B) what	5. (D) the reason why	6. (C) which
		7. (A) who	8. (D) with whom	9. (B) whose	10. (A) that	11. (B) which	12. (C) in which
► Error Recognition p.86	🖉	1. (1) that		2. (1) that → what			
	🖉	1. (5) that		2. (5) that → who			
► Unit Review p.88	🖉	1. ❶ 선행사	❷ 관용 용법	❶ I couldn't find what they hid.		❷ Whale is to mammal what shark is to fish.	
	🖉	2. ❶ 제한적 용법	❷ 계속적 용법	❶ She has two daughters who are programmers.		❷ She has two daughters, who are programmers.	
	🖉	3. ❶ whcih 앞	❷ 문장 맨 끝	❶ He saw the bird of which she is speaking.		❷ He saw the bird which she is speaking of.	
UNIT 3 p.92 ► Exercise 1	🖉	1. that	2. X	3. but	4. whoever	5. X	

▶ Exercise 2	🖉	1. Tell me anything you want.	2. Is this the right seat you reserved?	3. I will give this money to whoever wins.		
▶ Exercise 3	🖉	1. who	2. whom[that/X]	3. which[that/X]	4. which[that]	5. which[that]	6. Whichever
▶ Sentence completion p.94	🖉	1. (A) that	2. (C) who	3. (B) who	4. (B) which	5. (D) who is	6. (C) whom
		7. (C) than	8. (A) as	9. (D) whichever	10. (D) No matter whom	11. (C) anyone who	12. (B) what
▶ Error Recognition p.96	🖉	1. (5) but	2. (5) but → than				
	🖉	1. (3) Whomever	2. (3) Whomever → Whichever / Whatever				
▶ Unit Review p.98	🖉	1. ❶ The present (that) you gave me yesterday was awesome. ❷ You can buy the books (that are) on the shelf.					
	🖉	2. ❶ as ❷ but					
		❶ There are as many flowers as you want.		❷ The polar bear is bigger than the brown bear is.			
	🖉	3. ❶ 모든, 어떠한 ❷ 양보					
		❶ He would buy whichever belt he wants.		❷ Whatever(=No matter what) you say, I would go my own way.			

UNIT 4 p.102

▶ Exercise 1	🖉	1. when	2. in which	3. where	4. why	5. However	
▶ Exercise 2	🖉	1. This is the cave where Paleolithic humans lived.	2. It is impossible to predict the exact date they will finish the work.	3. Now is the time when you can try anything.		
▶ Exercise 3	🖉	1. where	2. which	3. why	4. in	5. why	6. where
▶ Sentence completion p.104	🖉	1. (A) X	2. (B) why	3. (C) when	4. (A) that	5. (C) in which	6. (A) X
		7. (D) the reason	8. (A) X	9. (C) when	10. (A) X	11. (A) X	12. (C) wherever
▶ Error Recognition p.106	🖉	1. (2) where	2. (2) where → when				
	🖉	1. (5) how	2. (5) how → however				
▶ Unit Review p.108	🖉	1. ❷ where ❺ that ❻ 제한적 ❼ 계속적					
		➡ I don't know the time when she arrived.					
	🖉	2. ➡ I understand the reason (why) you don't like this.					
	🖉	3. ➡ I have visited (the place) where they lived.					
	🖉	4. ❶ 관계부사 + ever ❷ why ➡ Whenever we meet, we go to the cafe.					
TOSEL 실전문제 5	🖉	1. (B) whose	2. (C) which	3. (A) that	4. (B) what	5. (D) to whom	6. (D) which
		7. (C) Whoever	8. (B) whom	9. (A) X	10. (C) when	11. (A) X	12. (A) why
	🖉	1. (2) which → where	2. (1) who → which, that		3. (1) what is	4. (4) whom
		5. (5) use it	6. (2) what				

CHAPTER 6
p.116

UNIT 1 p.120

▶ Exercise 1	🖉	1. save	2. prepare	3. wash	4. were	5. had	
▶ Exercise 2	🖉	1. If that cat cries, I will feed it.	2. If Sarah won, she would feel better.	3. If I were you, I would not give up.		
▶ Exercise 3	🖉	1. graduates	2. were	3. thinks	4. would receive	5. run	6. apologize
▶ Sentence completion p.122	🖉	1. (B) drops	2. (B) don't eat	3. (D) will go	4. (D) should follow	5. (C) could prevent	6. (C) were
		7. (C) could	8. (C) Anybody who	9. (A) had best	10. (D) would rather	11. (A) as it were	12. (A) study
▶ Error Recognition p.124	🖉	1. (5) are	2. (5) are → were				
	🖉	1. (5) to play	2. (5) to play → play				
▶ Unit Review p.126	🖉	1. ❶ 현재 ❷ 미래					
		❶ If it rains tomorrow, I will not go to the library.		❷ I suggest that you (should) summarize your report.			
		❸ She exercises regularly lest she (should) lose her health.					
	🖉	2. ❶ 현재 사실의 반대 ❷ 실현 불가능한 미래					
		❶ If I were you, I would hire the man.		❷ If you would give a reply, I would appreciate it.			
	🖉	3. ❶ You had better accept the criticism.		❷ She is, as it were, an AI.			

UNIT 2 p.130

▶ Exercise 1	🖉	1. have received	2. been	3. could	4. had	5. lived	
▶ Exercise 2	🖉	1. If you had come, you would have been surprised.	2. If I had become a teacher, I would have taught science.	3. If Grace had moved, she would have found a new job.		
▶ Exercise 3	🖉	1. known	2. written	3. taken	4. been	5. met	6. run

Sentence completion p.132	1. (B) we had known	2. (B) hadn't given up	3. (D) would have shown	4. (A) would have shot	5. (A) would have told	6. (D) would have earned
	7. (C) had dreamed	8. (C) If I had brushed	9. (D) would have gone	10. (A) could have finished	11. (A) could have slept	12. (D) should have received

Error Recognition p.134	1. (5) haven't	2. (5) haven't → hadn't
	1. (2) has modified	2. (2) has modified → has been modified

Unit Review p.136

1. ❶ 과거 사실

➔ ❶ If the weather had not been good, I would have stayed at home. ➔ ❷ If I had not studied hard, I would have enjoyed the holidays. ➔ ❸ If he had not been busy, he would have visited the place.

2. ➔ If Gina could have finished her work, we should have invited her.

UNIT 3 p.140

Exercise 1	1. be	2. marry	3. woke	4. would	5. as if

Exercise 2	1. If it had not been cloudy yesterday, it wouldn't be windy today.	2. It is time we went home.	3. I wish I were a scientist.

Exercise 3	1. be	2. finish	3. forget	4. known	5. remembers	6. are

Sentence completion p.142	1. (B) had	2. (A) be	3. (A) had	4. (C) yesterday	5. (C) this morning	6. (B) arrived
	7. (C) they were	8. (A) listen	9. (D) If only	10. (B) liked	11. (C) forgotten	12. (B) have

Error Recognition p.144	1. (3) are	2. (3) are → is
	1. (5) went	2. (5) went → gone

Unit Review p.146

1. ❶ 다른

❶ If Peter spoke Spanish, he would have interpreted for me. ❷ If you had used this mechanism, you would figure out the poblem now.

2. ❶ It is time you did something.
= It is time you should do something.
= It is time for you to do something.

❷ I wish he were a sensible boy.

❸ I wish my granfather had not worked a lot. ❹ Alex acts as if he were a king.

UNIT 4 p.150

Exercise 1	1. Were	2. Had	3. Should	4. to	5. A brave man

Exercise 2	1. Were I taller, I would be a basketball player.	2. If it were not for her, you would not be late.	3. We could have accomplished it with her teaching.

Exercise 3	1. Should	2. Were	3. Had	4. Had	5. gone	6. were

Sentence completion p.152	1. (B) Had we	2. (A) Had he	3. (D) Were	4. (C) Had they known	5. (D) Should	6. (B) If we had
	7. (D) Had they been	8. (C) If I took	9. (D) A student who	10. (A) Suppose	11. (B) Provided	12. (B) could

Error Recognition p.154	1. (5) going	2. (5) going → gone
	1. (4) Not had he	2. (4) Not had he → If he hadn't [Had he not]

Unit Review p.156

1. ❶ If의 조건절 ❷ 도치 ❸ 일반동사의 가정법 과거 ❹ 도치

❶ Were you in the department store, you would meet me. ❷ Had I watched the news, I would have understood the subject.

❸ Should I be alone, I would be sad.

2. ❶ Providing[Provided] that you frame a story, you may start writing. ❷ If it had not been for the reference books, I would not have understood the math formula.

❸ Had it not been for the reference bookes, I would not have understood the math formula. ❹ But[Except] for the reference books, I would not have understood the math formula.

❺ Without the reference books, I would not have understood the math formula.

TOSEL 실전문제 6	1. (A) be	2. (C) were	3. (D) would rather	4. (D) would have started	5. (C) had married	6. (C) have been
	7. (C) had enrolled	8. (D) was done	9. (A) hadn't spent	10. (B) Should you	11. (B) Provided	12. (C) Had it
	1. (3) as it was → as it were			2. (5) have → have been		
	3. (4) Did you do	4. (5) did not	5. (1) had looked	6. (4) participated		